Java 17 Backend Development

Design backend systems using Spring Boot, Docker, Kafka, Eureka, Redis, and Tomcat

AF668149

Elara Drevyn

Published by: GitforGits

Publisher: Sonal Dhandre

www.gitforgits.com

support@gitforgits.com

Printed in India

First Printing: December 2024

ISBN: 978-81-979504-5-2

Cover Design by: Kitten Publishing

Prologue

I know many Java professionals who struggle with bridging the gap between knowing the language fundamentals and writing a production-ready backend. They often find themselves grappling with configuration headaches, performance bottlenecks, and advanced frameworks that appear daunting. I decided to write this book because I've seen these problems time and again. Time and again, I saw talented developers trying to figure out how to adopt microservices, orchestrate containers, or integrate messaging systems, all while staying within deadlines and avoiding excessive complexity.

As I worked on various enterprise projects, I realized that certain patterns repeatedly emerged—connecting to databases with JPA or Hibernate, caching data, deploying with Tomcat or containers, managing configurations in dynamic environments, and ensuring proper testing strategies. There was a clear demand for concrete, step-by-step explanations. Colleagues expressed a clear need for guidance on handling concurrency, implementing security measures, and debugging errors in distributed services. Many felt overwhelmed by the number of libraries and the fast-paced changes in the ecosystem.

I'm sharing my experiences in a direct manner, focusing on how developers can utilize Java 17 effectively for server-side tasks. Each chapter tackles a specific need, from building REST endpoints to handling microservices communications. I show realistic tasks like setting up continuous integration, orchestrating containers, or installing caching solutions. I don't just present theoretical knowledge. I blend real application code with relevant concepts, not ignore them. My background in client-facing platforms convinced me that pushing code to production safely is just as important as writing elegant logic. I devote significant time to explaining testing, debugging, and the final mile of deployment.

While writing, I imagined a Java developer who has wrestled with half-baked solutions or incomplete instructions. I wanted them to see a cohesive path from the first lines of code to a reliable production environment. Throughout this book, I've deliberately chosen language that is accessible and real-world examples that are easy to understand. You will gain the confidence to piece everything together, no matter the size of the system they are creating. Java 17's new features enhance maintainability and performance, and this book shows how they seamlessly integrate into modern backend practices.

"Approach backend development with renewed enthusiasm and ability to tackle emerging challenges head-on"

- Elara Drevyn

Content

Preface

This book offers beginners and backend developers with practical guidance on developing robust server-side applications with Java 17. Each chapter is structured around hands-on examples, real-world challenges, and step-by-step solutions tailored to Java professionals aiming to elevate their expertise in backend systems. It seamlessly transitions through essential development phases, covering everything from foundational elements like object-oriented design and basic REST endpoints to advanced microservices architecture and container orchestration. It covers everything from wiring up databases with Hibernate to managing asynchronous communication with Apache Kafka and securing endpoints with Spring Security. You will gain insight into caching strategies with Redis and diving into techniques to boost performance and reduce database load. It also covers Spring Cloud concepts like Eureka for service discovery and Config Server for centralized management, showing how microservices function cohesively.

The book also covers testing and debugging topics, highlighting modern tools and practices such as JUnit, Mockito, integration tests, and distributed tracing. The book clearly encourages consistent coding standards, efficient concurrency patterns, and a layered approach for verifying logic. As the book moves forward, it clearly illustrates how to maintain code quality and automate deployment workflows using continuous integration and delivery pipelines. Towards the book's end, you will know how to run Java 17 backend applications in production environments, and you will be applying best practices for logging, monitoring, security, and scalability. You will witness how all of these pieces fit together in a coherent ecosystem, whether they are deploying on Tomcat or containerizing with Docker.

In this book you will learn to:

- Set up RESTful APIs and data mappings.
- Use Spring Security for robust user authentication and role-based access control.
- Employ Redis caching techniques to offload databases and enhance performance.
- Integrate Kafka to establish asynchronous, high-throughput communication among microservices.
- Adopt Spring Cloud tools for configuration, discovery, and gateway-based microservice architectures.
- Employ Docker containerization for portable deployments across environments.
- Construct CI/CD pipelines to automate testing, building, and delivery of microservices.
- Conduct thorough integration testing with real databases, brokers, and external dependencies.

- Use debugging tools, logs, and distributed tracing to isolate production issues.
- Optimize concurrency, resource usage, and monitoring to handle large-scale backend demands.

GitforGits

Prerequisites

This book is for Java developers, Spring developers, Spring Boot Programmers, web developers, and full-stack developers, as well as anyone interested in exploring the world of Java to improve the back-end of enterprise applications. You'll need some hands-on experience with Java 17 to get the most out of this book.

Codes Usage

Are you in need of some helpful code examples to assist you in your programming and documentation? Look no further! Our book offers a wealth of supplemental material, including code examples and exercises.

Not only is this book here to aid you in getting your job done, but you have our permission to use the example code in your programs and documentation. However, please note that if you are reproducing a significant portion of the code, we do require you to contact us for permission.

But don't worry, using several chunks of code from this book in your program or answering a question by citing our book and quoting example code does not require permission. But if you do choose to give credit, an attribution typically includes the title, author, publisher, and ISBN. For example, " Java 17 Backend Development by Elara Drevyn".

If you are unsure whether your intended use of the code examples falls under fair use or the permissions outlined above, please do not hesitate to reach out to us at support@gitforgits.com.

We are happy to assist and clarify any concerns.

Acknowledgement

I owe a tremendous debt of gratitude to GitforGits, for their unflagging enthusiasm and wise counsel throughout the entire process of writing this book. Their knowledge and careful editing helped make sure the piece was useful for people of all reading levels and comprehension skills. In addition, I'd like to thank everyone involved in the publishing process for their efforts in making this book a reality. Their efforts, from copyediting to advertising, made the project what it is today.

Finally, I'd like to express my gratitude to everyone who has shown me unconditional love and encouragement throughout my life. Their support was crucial to the completion of this book. I appreciate your help with this endeavour and your continued interest in my career.

CHAPTER 1: INTRODUCTION TO JAVA 17 AND BACKEND DEVELOPMENT

Understanding Java 17 Features

The Java programming language has traveled a long and interesting path since its inception in the mid-1990s. An initial release of Java 1.0 arrived around 1995 with a promise of "write once, run anywhere" that captured the attention of developers who sought more portability in their projects. It began as something that could power applets inside browsers, then gradually found its place in server-side applications, enterprise systems, and various kinds of backend services. Over time, Java 2, Java 5, and later Java 8 introduced new syntactic sugar, improved concurrency models, and functional-style programming through lambdas and streams. By the time Java 11 came around, developers noticed a more rapid release cadence, with new major versions emerging every six months instead of every few years. This shift also introduced the concept of Long-Term Support (LTS) versions, where selected releases receive extended support and stability guarantees. Moving through Java 12, Java 13, and onward, incremental improvements enhanced overall language ergonomics. Java 14, Java 15, and Java 16 added pattern matching, better switch expressions, text blocks, and other features that simplified working with data. By the time we reach Java 17, the community finds a major LTS milestone that many consider to be a sensible baseline for modern server-side coding. Java has not stopped evolving with 17, as more recent versions like Java 18, Java 19, Java 20, Java 21, Java 22, and the emerging Java 23 continue to refine features, expand pattern matching, enhance virtual threads, and integrate new APIs. Each passing version encourages developers to write more expressive, more secure, and more maintainable code, while retaining backward compatibility for older projects that need stability and continuity.

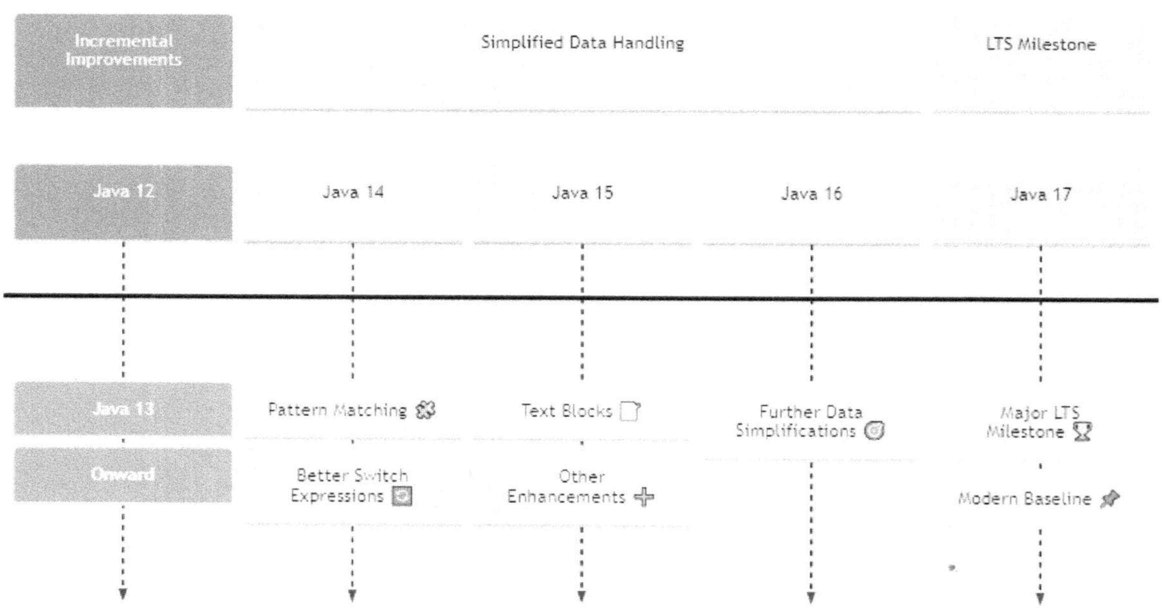

Fig 1.1 Java Version Evolution

A large portion of the Java community gravitates toward Java 17 for several practical reasons, primarily because it represents a stable LTS release that many enterprises trust for building and maintaining production services. With the rapid pace of Java's six-month release cycle, some releases are not supported for a long period, so enterprises often wait for these LTS versions to ensure that their codebases have a stable foundation for the next several years. Java 17 stands out as a version that introduced features designed to improve productivity, clarity, and maintainability. It also removed some outdated components from the language's standard library that had been marked as deprecated for a while, thereby trimming unnecessary baggage. By choosing Java 17, backend developers gain access to a more modern syntax and gain the ability to leverage improved garbage collection algorithms, better performance, and more efficient runtime behavior compared to older LTS versions like Java 11 or even Java 8. The community appreciates that Java 17 is considered a sensible default for many greenfield projects and also a worthwhile upgrade for existing codebases seeking modern language features and enhancements that align nicely with backend development needs.

The salient attributes of Java 17 go beyond just having LTS status. It refines many ideas introduced in recent releases and stabilizes them for long-term use. Among the compelling features are sealed classes and records, which represent new ways of shaping data models and controlling class hierarchies. Java developers who build large and complex backend systems often appreciate having better tools to design APIs, control inheritance, and simplify data handling. Sealed classes, for instance, make it possible to create class hierarchies that are intentionally closed. This means a developer can declare a base class and strictly define which subclasses are permitted to extend it. By doing so, the shape of the hierarchy becomes clearer and more stable, preventing unexpected types from appearing in places they don't belong. For backend code that often deals with complex domain models, microservices architectures, or intricate business logic, sealed classes help reduce confusion by clearly stating the intended set of allowed subclasses. This leads to more predictable behavior, easier reasoning about code, and fewer nasty surprises when integrating separate parts of a large system.

A related feature that has gained popularity is records, which represent a compact and transparent way to define classes that are primarily about holding data. Traditional Java required developers to write verbose classes with getters, setters, equals, hashCode, and toString methods to manage data entities. Records cut down on this boilerplate by automatically generating those common methods while ensuring that the defined class remains immutable. By using records, a backend developer can focus on describing the shape of the data rather than being bogged down by repetitive code. This immutable and data-focused design fits perfectly with microservices, as services often pass around small data objects representing messages, entities retrieved from databases, or configuration values. Records make it easier to ensure that data flows through the system in a safe and predictable manner. Backend developers who have dealt with frameworks that require plain old Java objects (POJOs) can appreciate how records simplify and clarify that code.

The improvements in Java 17 are not limited to just these headline features. Over the many versions leading to Java 17, the language introduced pattern matching for instance-of checks, which simplifies code that performs type checks on objects. Prior to this, developers would write verbose code to cast objects after verifying their type. Pattern matching reduces the friction by extracting a variable of the matched type automatically, making the code shorter and more readable. For backend systems that handle diverse data inputs from various sources, having cleaner type checks improves maintainability. Another useful enhancement involves text blocks, which were stabilized in earlier versions but now feel like a standard tool. Text blocks let developers write multi-line strings cleanly, which can be helpful for embedding queries, templates, or configuration snippets directly in code without a bunch of escaping and concatenation. Backend code often needs to handle SQL queries, JSON payloads, or XML templates, and text blocks make it easier to read and maintain these kinds of inline resources.

The reason these features matter so much in backend programming comes down to productivity, reliability, and readability. A backend often deals with complex systems integrating databases, cache layers, microservices, messaging queues, and security frameworks. In such environments, developers want language features that help express intent more directly without generating cognitive overhead. Sealed classes help define strict hierarchies that protect certain internal implementations from being misused or extended by unknown classes. Records enable straightforward data carriers that fit nicely with APIs returning JSON or XML payloads. Pattern matching speeds up and clarifies code paths that differ based on object type. Text blocks allow embedding data structures or large strings directly into code without error-prone escapes. Taken as a whole, these improvements mean that backend code can evolve more gracefully, remain more maintainable over time, and communicate intent more clearly to future maintainers of the system.

An important aspect of moving to Java 17 is understanding that it represents a point in the language's evolution where many newer features have matured enough to be used widely in production environments. Developers who might have been hesitant to jump from earlier versions finally have a stable and well-supported platform. By the time Java 17 became an LTS release, its features had been polished through earlier preview stages, which allowed the community to provide feedback and the language designers to refine their approach. This collaborative process ensured that features like sealed classes and records not only feel stable but also integrate well with the existing ecosystem of libraries and frameworks. When building backend services, a developer often relies on frameworks like Spring, Micronaut, or Quarkus, and these frameworks quickly adapt to new Java versions. With Java 17 at the core, these technologies can unlock new ways of writing cleaner beans, entities, and configurations, which in turn provides a better development experience.

By focusing on how these features improve backend programming, it becomes apparent that Java's evolution is directly addressing the needs of modern server-side workloads. A backend system in 2024 might be deployed to a container orchestrated by Kubernetes, integrate with distributed caches like Redis, and communicate asynchronously with messaging systems. Such complexity demands languages and runtimes that not only perform well but also simplify the development process. Java 17 accomplishes this by reducing boilerplate, giving developers more expressive constructs, and allowing more confident refactoring. When sealed classes define which implementations are allowed, there is a reduced risk of accidentally introducing classes that break the intended architecture. When records model data carriers, the code becomes more concise and less prone to human error when writing repetitive constructors or equals methods. When pattern matching is used, the code path for handling different object types feels natural and direct. When text blocks are included, embedding external data inside the code is cleaner and less error-prone.

In practice, these enhancements empower teams to build and maintain backends that remain adaptable. As projects grow and change, the language encourages more robust design patterns. Rather than forcing developers to write repetitive code, Java 17 encourages more declarative data modeling. Rather than leaving class hierarchies open-ended and prone to unintended subclassing, sealed classes encourage designers to think upfront about which classes should participate. Rather than relying on external libraries to reduce boilerplate, records provide a first-class feature right out of the language itself. These choices reflect a shifting approach to backend development where developers want to spend more time addressing business requirements and less time wrestling with tedious code patterns.

By adopting Java 17, a backend team demonstrates a commitment to using a modern and stable platform that benefits from the lessons learned over multiple iterations of the language. This platform integrates nicely with the entire Java ecosystem, including build tools, dependency injection frameworks, ORM libraries, and monitoring utilities. It also serves as a springboard for moving forward as new versions appear. Subsequent releases up to Java 23 and beyond continue to refine pattern matching, introduce new language constructs, and optimize the runtime. Each new feature can be seen as building upon the stable foundation that Java 17 established.

A backend written in Java 17 can still run in environments that have been in place for years, but it can now evolve using these more modern constructs. It can interact seamlessly with container-based deployments, leverage cloud-native technologies, and integrate emerging architectural patterns like event-driven microservices. The language's syntax and semantics help developers write code that is both more elegant and more transparent, making the lives of those who build and maintain backend systems much more pleasant.

Role of Backend Development

An application's backend is often described as the engine room or the hidden machinery that powers various functionalities, data flows, and logic behind the scenes. It never takes center stage visually, but it continuously works under the hood to process requests, store and retrieve information, and provide consistent results that can be displayed on devices or browser windows. It can be understood as a set of interconnected systems that coordinate with each other to ensure smooth and efficient operations. These systems typically include server-side frameworks, APIs, databases, caching layers, authentication services, message brokers, load balancers, and various integration points for external systems. Each part contributes to making entire applications more reliable, scalable, and secure. The user interface might provide a pleasant experience, but it is the backend that ensures data correctness, stable performance, and the capacity to handle large volumes of traffic as the application grows.

A server-side framework is often the backbone of the backend application, acting as a container for code that processes requests and dispatches them to proper handlers. It can provide structured ways to route requests, implement middleware layers, and manage application states. Another significant element involves APIs, which define clear contracts that clients can call to perform operations on the system's data. These APIs generally follow standardized practices like REST or GraphQL, making it simpler for different services to communicate in a consistent manner. Databases are another essential piece, responsible for persisting data over time. Backend systems typically choose relational databases like MySQL or PostgreSQL for structured data, or NoSQL solutions like MongoDB or Cassandra for more flexible storage patterns. The choice of database can impact performance, scalability, and the overall approach to organizing data, so developers often think carefully about which technology best suits their needs.

A caching layer is commonly used to reduce the load on the database by storing frequently accessed data in memory. By retrieving data from a cache like Redis, the backend can respond faster and handle more concurrent traffic. This improves overall performance because the system spends less time fetching the same data repeatedly from persistent storage. Beyond caching, other specialized tools such as message queues or event streaming platforms like Apache Kafka help the backend distribute tasks or events among different components, improving resilience and fault tolerance. The backend may also coordinate with third-party APIs or services, integrating functionalities like payment processing, email delivery, file storage, or analytics. When these various elements align well, the backend becomes a flexible and powerful infrastructure that supports the entire application's needs.

A backend developer's responsibilities often revolve around building, maintaining, and optimizing these underlying systems that the frontend depends upon. An individual in this role writes server-side code that runs on machines dedicated to handling incoming network requests. Such code might involve parsing requests, applying business rules, querying databases, and producing structured responses. This can involve analyzing data models, writing database queries, and designing schemas that represent the entities and relationships within the domain. A backend developer might create REST endpoints to retrieve a list of products, insert a new order, update customer information, or remove outdated records. By carefully designing these endpoints, the backend professional shapes how data is accessed, how errors are handled, and how clients must interact with the system.

A backend developer also handles security measures to ensure that only authorized individuals or processes can access certain parts of the system. Tasks might include implementing authentication mechanisms, where users sign in with credentials or tokens, and authorization logic, which decides what actions those authenticated users are allowed to perform. This can be accomplished by integrating frameworks like Spring Security for Java-based projects or by writing custom middleware to handle JWT tokens, API keys, or session cookies. Ensuring the system is not vulnerable to common attacks, such as SQL injection or cross-site scripting through improper input handling, is part of backend responsibility as well.

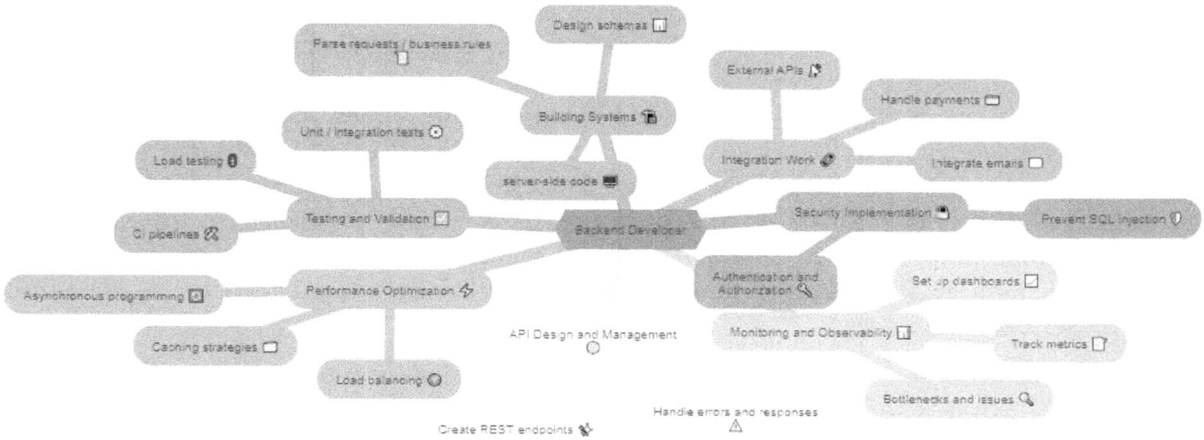

Fig 1.2 Backend Developer Responsibilities

A backend developer often embraces performance optimization. This can mean adding appropriate caching strategies, tuning database queries, or adjusting server configurations to handle more concurrent requests. By analyzing metrics like response times, memory usage, or CPU load, developers can pinpoint bottlenecks and refactor code or data models to improve throughput. This might involve selecting the right indexing strategies for databases, using asynchronous programming techniques for handling intensive I/O operations, or load balancing traffic across multiple servers to prevent a single node from becoming overwhelmed. By ensuring that the backend can scale as the application grows, the developer creates an environment where increased user demands can be met gracefully.

A backend developer also takes care of integration work. Perhaps the system needs to communicate with a payment provider to process online transactions. The developer would design a secure communication channel, handle potential errors like declined cards or insufficient funds, and store transaction results so they can be referenced later. If the application needs to send email notifications, the developer would integrate with an email service, format messages, handle delivery failures, and record logs for auditing. By writing code that gracefully deals with external APIs and services, the backend developer ensures that the application can reliably use external functionality as part of its workflow.

A critical part of a backend developer's job involves testing and verifying that the system behaves as intended. This can mean writing unit tests that check individual functions, integration tests that validate how different parts of the system work together, or load tests that simulate heavy traffic conditions. These practices help confirm that the system responds correctly to both expected and unexpected inputs. They also encourage creating code that is more modular and easier to maintain. The developer can use continuous integration tools to automatically run tests whenever changes are made, catching issues early before they reach production. Such care leads to higher-quality software that can handle real-world conditions more robustly.

A backend developer frequently collaborates with other team members, such as frontend developers, database administrators, DevOps engineers, and system architects. This collaboration ensures that everyone shares a common understanding of how data flows through the system and what formats are expected. If a frontend developer needs a new endpoint for displaying recommended products, the backend developer coordinates with that individual to define the request and response structure. If the operations team needs to deploy the backend into a containerized environment, the backend developer might help by ensuring that the application reads its configuration from environment variables or handles graceful shutdown signals. This teamwork helps keep the system coherent and prevents misunderstandings that could lead to errors or performance issues.

A backend developer also stays current with evolving technologies, frameworks, and best practices. The world of software development changes fast, and backend developers are expected to keep an eye on emerging trends, performance improvements in newer languages or frameworks, or even updated versions of tools they already use. By reading release notes, attending local meetups, experimenting with sample projects, or reviewing official documentation, backend developers remain prepared to adopt better solutions as their projects evolve. This ongoing learning helps them write code that aligns well with current standards, security guidelines, and industry practices.

A backend developer's role can also involve setting up observability and monitoring tools. Instead of treating the application as a black box, it is helpful to track metrics, logs, and traces to understand how the system behaves in production environments. By integrating with monitoring systems like Prometheus, Grafana, or Elastic Stack, a developer can set up dashboards that reveal usage patterns, slow endpoints, or error spikes. This visibility helps in proactive maintenance, allowing quick detection and resolution of issues before end users are seriously impacted. Over time, the data gleaned from logs and metrics can walkthrough improvements in system design, capacity planning, or selecting which parts of the codebase need refactoring.

A backend developer also takes care when handling data migrations and schema changes. If the database schema needs to evolve due to new business requirements, the backend developer plans how to introduce these changes without causing downtime or data loss. Techniques like backward-compatible schema changes, rolling updates, and carefully planned indexing can ensure that the system continues running smoothly even as underlying data structures evolve. This adaptability is essential since applications often change as they grow, adding features, supporting new workflows, or integrating with different external systems.

The backend developer often relies on automated pipelines to build, test, and deploy the code into various environments, such as development, staging, and production. By using tools like Jenkins, GitHub Actions, or GitLab CI/CD, the developer can ensure that every code change passes through a consistent process. This includes running tests, performing static analysis, scanning for security vulnerabilities, and packaging the application for deployment. By automating these tasks, the backend developer reduces manual work and human error, improving overall efficiency and making it easier to respond to new requirements or bug fixes quickly. It also encourages a continuous improvement cycle, where incremental changes can be delivered more frequently without sacrificing quality.

An additional responsibility for a backend developer involves handling errors, edge cases, and unexpected conditions gracefully. A robust backend does not crash or return confusing errors if it encounters malformed input, temporary database outages, or rate-limited third-party APIs. Instead, it recovers gracefully, returns helpful error messages, retries operations if needed, and logs problems for further investigation. This resilience improves user satisfaction by avoiding extended downtimes or lost requests. It also helps developers diagnose problems more easily, as well-structured error logs make troubleshooting more straightforward.

A backend developer's role is highly varied, touching on system architecture, data modeling, security, performance tuning, and tooling. By weaving together all these components, the backend developer delivers an application layer that others can depend on, whether those others are frontend developers creating user interfaces or automated systems consuming APIs for integration. This role continues to expand as the industry grows more interconnected, data-driven, and service-oriented. Although it might remain less visible than frontend work, the importance of a solid backend persists, enabling modern applications to serve their users reliably, securely, and efficiently.

Overview of Backend Technologies

Spring and Spring Boot

A powerful and popular foundation for building backend services in the Java ecosystem is Spring, which provides a flexible structure for wiring together different parts of an application. It offers dependency injection, aspect-oriented programming, and modular components that simplify code maintenance. A large portion of modern backend development with Java revolves around Spring Boot, an opinionated framework sitting on top of Spring that streamlines project setup and configuration. By using Spring Boot starters, automatic configurations, and embedded application servers, it becomes much easier to get a service running with minimal boilerplate. A backend engineer can define beans, wire them together through annotations, and launch a production-ready application without wasting time on repetitive setup steps. In environments where time to market and reliability matter, Spring Boot helps deliver a more organized development experience. It also supports integration with other libraries, ensuring that the backend can seamlessly adopt technologies like Hibernate ORM or connect to external APIs. Through its convention-over-configuration philosophy, Spring Boot creates an environment where developers can quickly adapt new patterns or incorporate additional modules as the application grows more complex, all while maintaining a unified codebase that remains readable and approachable.

Hibernate ORM

A fundamental responsibility of many backend systems is to manage data persistence, which generally means interacting with relational databases to store, retrieve, and update information. Hibernate ORM provides a robust framework that abstracts away the underlying SQL queries, enabling developers to work directly with Java objects rather than manually writing database statements. By using annotations to define entities, relationships, and mappings, Hibernate streamlines the process of persisting complex data structures to tables. This approach leads to cleaner and more maintainable code, especially as the schema evolves over time. With Hibernate, developers often rely on the Java Persistence API (JPA) specifications, which ensure a consistent set of interfaces and annotations to manage entity states, transactions, and lazy loading. For a backend application that must run complex queries, handle large datasets, or maintain intricate associations between entities, Hibernate provides a stable foundation that can improve productivity. By eliminating repetitive SQL handling, it lets engineers focus on higher-level tasks, such as refining domain models or ensuring that data access patterns are efficient enough for production workloads. The direct integration of Hibernate with Spring Boot makes the process of wiring repositories, data sources, and transactional boundaries even more convenient, ensuring that backend developers can focus on business logic instead of infrastructure details.

RESTful APIs

A key responsibility of a backend system is to provide interfaces that other services, clients, or devices can call to perform operations or retrieve data. RESTful APIs, built on HTTP and stateless principles, represent a common way of achieving this. A developer defines endpoints that accept requests via URLs, handle payloads in formats like JSON, and respond with data that the caller can parse. REST provides a language-agnostic way for different parts of an ecosystem to interact. By following best practices such as resource-oriented design, proper use of HTTP methods, and meaningful status codes, a backend team can create APIs that are easy to understand and extend. Frameworks like Spring Web MVC simplify the process of defining controllers, mapping URLs to methods, handling request parameters, and formatting responses. When integrated with Spring Boot, setting up RESTful endpoints can be done with a few annotations and a small amount of code, letting developers focus on the underlying logic instead of HTTP plumbing. By relying on RESTful patterns, the backend can easily support multiple frontend clients, mobile apps, and even other backend systems that need to integrate data. This approach leads to better maintainability, reuse, and scalability over time, as changes to one component do not necessarily break others if the API contracts remain stable.

Security, Caching, Messaging, and Microservices

A complete backend system often incorporates more specialized technologies to address common enterprise needs. Spring Security, for instance, provides a flexible approach to adding authentication and authorization layers, protecting sensitive endpoints, and enforcing role-based access control. Instead of manually handling user credentials or token validation, a developer can rely on Spring Security's pluggable architecture, which integrates neatly into the Spring Boot environment. For improved performance, caching solutions like Redis help avoid repeated database queries by storing frequently accessed information in memory, reducing latency and offloading work from the database. In scenarios where applications must communicate asynchronously, message brokers like Apache Kafka come into play. Kafka allows backend services to publish and consume event streams, enabling features like real-time notifications, event-driven processing, and robust decoupling between components. For larger systems that benefit from distributed architectures, microservices concepts and tools from the Spring Cloud ecosystem help break monolithic applications into smaller, independently deployable services. This enables teams to scale particular components more easily, roll out updates without affecting the entire system, and adopt patterns like service discovery, centralized configuration, load balancing, and fault tolerance. These additional technologies round out the backend capabilities, ensuring that the system can handle security, performance, messaging, and architectural complexity as the application grows. Each tool works hand-in-hand with the foundational frameworks like Spring and Hibernate, creating a unified environment for building sophisticated backend solutions that can adapt to evolving requirements.

Introduction to Book Application

Overview of GitforGits Project

A practical approach to learning complex backend concepts often involves immersing oneself in a realistic application that evolves over time. A helpful way to apply the lessons from the previous sections is to pick a project that models real-world needs and demonstrates how various tools, frameworks, and architectural principles fit together. The GitforGits project serves as such an example, offering a fictional environment where publishers, authors, and readers all come together around books that need to be organized, stored, retrieved, and delivered efficiently. An essential goal is to reveal how each part of the backend stack contributes to building a coherent, robust, and maintainable application that remains open to future changes. By selecting a domain that most individuals can relate to—managing books and related publishing tasks—this project bridges theoretical constructs with practical implementations. A backend focusing on publishing workflows might need to handle information about authors, store metadata for books and their versions, maintain user accounts for those who manage the publishing lifecycle, and provide a secure environment for authenticated individuals to perform operations like adding new titles or updating descriptions. A publishing workflow often demands structured data storage for cataloging books, scalable endpoints for retrieving book lists or searching for authors, security features to ensure that only authorized users can modify content, caching strategies to serve frequently accessed items more quickly, and possibly integrations with messaging systems to send notifications when new titles become available. Each piece of technology introduced throughout the chapters will find a role in bringing these capabilities to life, ensuring that learning never remains abstract.

An early stage of the GitforGits project might focus on simply standing up a Spring Boot application that can store book records in a relational database via Hibernate. This initial groundwork not only introduces fundamental concepts like configuring data sources or creating entity classes for persistent storage but also prepares the field for more advanced features. As the chapters advance, the project might incorporate user management so that individuals with different roles—such as authors, editors, or administrators—can log in and perform allowed actions. The introduction of authentication and authorization mechanisms will illustrate how Spring Security fits naturally into this environment, controlling access to endpoints while ensuring that sensitive operations, like publishing new editions or modifying pricing details, remain restricted. By weaving in RESTful APIs, the project will demonstrate how to expose these capabilities so that web-based frontends or mobile clients can interact with the backend to browse available titles, filter by category, or fetch the latest releases. To improve performance and responsiveness under increasing loads, the project could integrate caching strategies with tools like Redis, ensuring that data frequently requested by users is served more swiftly, thus reducing both latency and server load. Taking these ideas further, messaging systems like Apache Kafka might come into play for asynchronous tasks such as notifying authors when their books hit certain sales thresholds, or syncing newly published titles to external partner catalogs. By applying microservices concepts, the GitforGits architecture could evolve from a single monolithic application into a collection of independent services that communicate through well-defined interfaces, enabling more rapid scaling, independent deployments, and finer-grained control over different parts of the publishing pipeline.

Tools and Concepts

A natural progression within the GitforGits project involves gradually layering complexity as more backend concepts are introduced. An early chapter might start by setting up a minimal Spring Boot application that can handle a simple request to list all known titles in a static catalog. Later, as understanding deepens, the project might incorporate a database by defining entity classes representing books, authors, and categories, along with repository interfaces that leverage Hibernate to translate Java operations into SQL queries. Such a step demonstrates how data moves from persistent storage to API responses with minimal manual code. Following that, the next layer might focus on user management and security, illustrating how to limit certain operations—like adding a new book—to authenticated publishers only. This integration reveals the interplay between standard technologies such as Spring Security and the existing stack, showing how authentication tokens, user credentials, and access rules work together. Gradually, the project might introduce performance enhancements, calling attention to how caching mechanisms reduce the time it takes to fetch frequently requested metadata, or how asynchronous messaging can handle tasks that do not need to be processed synchronously, thus freeing the application to handle more requests concurrently. By doing this incrementally, the GitforGits project becomes a story of continuous improvement—starting from a basic codebase and transforming it into a more sophisticated system prepared to handle real-world scenarios. Through adding RESTful endpoints, refining database queries, layering in testing strategies, and exploring containerization for deployment, the project will constantly evolve in complexity and capability. Each technological addition is tied back to practical motivations, such as improving user experience by speeding up response times, enhancing maintainability by organizing the code into logical modules, or ensuring scalability so that a surge in requests doesn't bring the system to its knees. By the end of this book, the GitforGits application will serve as a comprehensive demonstration of how a collection of backend technologies, principles, and practices can work harmoniously, inspiring developers to adapt and extend these patterns into their own professional projects.

Summary

This chapter gave a rundown of how the Java language has changed over time. It started out as a language focused on portability and applets, and then it added new features like functional features in versions like Java 8. It showed how each version added features that made developers more productive, offered better runtime efficiencies, and introduced constructs like sealed classes and records. These new features were described as solutions that simplified data modeling, enhanced code clarity, and encouraged maintainable architecture. The chapter also showed how Java 17's role as a long-term support release encouraged widespread adoption by enterprises seeking stability.

It also talked about backend development and how the layers of an application that you can't see handled data flows, security, integrations, and performance optimizations. It showed how developers dealt with tasks like structuring APIs, modeling databases, and ensuring the scalability and reliability of services. Then, it talked about the tools that shaped this backend environment, like Spring Boot, Hibernate, and RESTful APIs. Lastly, it introduced the GitforGits project, a fictional book publishing application designed to apply and reinforce the concepts learned. The project is designed to connect the theoretical stuff with the practical, and it gradually builds up a backend system.

Chapter 2: Setting up Development Environment

Installing Java Development Kit (JDK) 17

If you want a reliable backend development environment, you've got to start with properly installing a stable version of the JDK. A lot of people choose version 17 because of its characteristics. You can find a suitable Linux environment with a terminal and the necessary tools to configure system variables. A common approach is to use the default package repositories, as long as they have an updated JDK 17 package. If you're on Ubuntu or Debian, you can start by updating package lists and searching the repository for OpenJDK 17. This involves running a set of commands in the terminal, which might need admin permissions. If your distribution doesn't have JDK 17 packages, you can always download a tar.gz archive directly from adoptium.net or Oracle's official distribution sources. After extracting the archive, the system paths and environment variables can be adjusted so that the **java** and **javac** commands become globally accessible. A quick verification step confirms the successful installation. Without these steps, other components and build tools introduced in later sections will not integrate smoothly.

To get started with a practical demo, you'll need to check which repos have JDK 17 packages. On Ubuntu, you could run something like this:

```
sudo apt update
apt search openjdk-17
```

If **openjdk-17-jdk** is listed, installation proceeds with:

```
sudo apt install openjdk-17-jdk
```

After the installation completes, verifying that the new JDK is functional involves a few commands such as running:

```
java -version
```

should display something like **openjdk version "17.x.x"** confirming that the runtime works. Similarly, the below one:

```
javac -version
```

should indicate the compiler's version as 17. These verifications ensure that the correct commands are on the system PATH, and that the environment recognizes the intended JDK. In cases where multiple Java versions already exist, Debian-based systems use the **update-alternatives** mechanism to configure a preferred default. You can simply run:

```
sudo update-alternatives --config java
```

```
sudo update-alternatives --config javac
```

and select the appropriate Java 17 entries. If done correctly, the environment respects this selection for future terminal sessions.

A scenario where no suitable JDK 17 package is found in repositories might involve manually installing from a tarball. For example, a tar.gz archive named **openjdk-17_linux-x64_bin.tar.gz** is downloaded into the **~/Downloads** directory. Nowo here, the extraction of it to a system-level directory goes like as below:

```
cd ~/Downloads
tar -xvf openjdk-17_linux-x64_bin.tar.gz
sudo mkdir -p /usr/local/java
sudo mv jdk-17* /usr/local/java/jdk-17
```

This places all JDK files into **/usr/local/java/jdk-17**. At this point, setting environment variables ensures that all tools know where Java resides. Now here, adding the following lines to **~/.bashrc** (for Bash users) could look like:

```
export JAVA_HOME=/usr/local/java/jdk-17
export PATH=$JAVA_HOME/bin:$PATH
```

After saving, running:

```
source ~/.bashrc
```

applies the changes to the current session. If we check **java -version** and **javac -version** again, then it confirms that the installed JDK 17 is now active. If the output matches the expected versions, then the JDK is ready to be used by other tools like Maven, Gradle, or IDEs.

There is also a helpful test that involves creating a simple Java file and compiling it. If we create a file named **HelloWorld.java** in the home directory or a working folder, then it shows the environment in action. For instance, using a text editor like nano:

```
nano HelloWorld.java
```

Then adding the following lines:

```
public class HelloWorld {
```

```
    public static void main(String[] args) {
        System.out.println("Java 17 is working fine!");
    }
}
```

After saving and exiting the editor, the file then can be compiled with:

```
javac HelloWorld.java
```

If no errors appear, the compiler generates a **HelloWorld.class** file. And then running:

```
java HelloWorld
```

should print:

```
Java 17 is working fine!
```

This output verifies that the JDK's compiler and runtime are correctly installed, the PATH is set, and no conflicting Java versions interfere. Such a test, while simple, ensures that the rest of the environment configuration tasks proceed without unexpected issues.

Another consideration involves IDE integration. While integrated development environments like IntelliJ IDEA or Eclipse will be introduced in the next topics, having a working JDK beforehand ensures that these tools detect Java 17 automatically. The same applies when adding frameworks or build tools. For instance, when Maven is introduced, it will look for **JAVA_HOME** or rely on the default **java** command. If these are already set, configuring Maven or Gradle will be simpler. Similarly, when adopting Spring Boot, the initial project creation process involves compiling and running classes that depend on the JDK. Without these foundational steps, a developer might get stuck debugging environment issues rather than focusing on coding the backend application.

With Java now properly installed and verified, the environment is ready to support more advanced tooling. The next topics focus on adding integrated development environments, dependency managers, and frameworks to build a practical and production-grade backend application.

Setting up Eclipse IDE

First, make sure the Java environment is ready because Eclipse relies on the JDK you installed earlier. Just open your browser and go to *https://www.eclipse.org/downloads/* to find the latest stable release for Java developers. You'll see something like "Eclipse IDE for Java Developers" or another option for backend development if you scroll down the page. If you're using a 64-bit distribution, go for the 64-bit Linux version. Once you find a suitable installer, just copy the download link and head back to your terminal to download it. You could run a command similar to:

```
wget
https://download.eclipse.org/technology/epp/downloads/release/
2023-09/R/eclipse-inst-jre-linux64.tar.gz
```

(Replace the URL with the exact one from the website.) You then confirm that the tar.gz file downloaded successfully by listing files in your current directory. You should see something like:

eclipse-inst-jre-linux64.tar.gz.

Then, we will extract the archive by running:

```
tar -xvf eclipse-inst-jre-linux64.tar.gz
```

This command produces a directory called something like **eclipse-installer** or **eclipse-inst-jre-linux64**. You then enter that directory and look for an executable file named **eclipse-inst**. You may also need to add execute permissions by running:

```
chmod +x eclipse-inst
```

After adjusting permissions, you can start the installer with:

```
./eclipse-inst
```

Here, a graphical installer window will appear. You select "Eclipse IDE for Java Developers" from the list and follow the on-screen instructions. You pick an installation folder such as **/usr/local/eclipse** to keep things organized. After you confirm the installation steps, Eclipse is installed into that directory. If you wish to run it from anywhere on your system, you can create a symbolic link:

```
sudo ln -s /usr/local/eclipse/eclipse /usr/local/bin/eclipse
```

Next, type **eclipse** into the terminal now, it will launch the IDE. You then select a workspace directory where your code and projects will reside. When Eclipse starts, you can go to **Window > Preferences > Java > Installed JREs** to confirm that Eclipse detects your JDK 17. If no JDK appears, you can click "Add," choose "Standard VM," and browse to your JDK 17 directory. After saving these changes, Eclipse knows exactly which Java runtime to use.

Later, you can test the setup by creating a new Java project. You go to **File > New > Java Project**, enter a project name, and ensure that the Java version matches what you installed. After the project is created, you can right-click the **src** folder, select **New > Class**, and name it **TestEclipseIntegration**. You also simply add a sample code as below:

```
public class TestEclipseIntegration {
    public static void main(String[] args) {
        System.out.println("Eclipse and JDK 17 are configured
correctly.");
    }
}
```

You run it by selecting **Run > Run As > Java Application** or by clicking the green run icon on the toolbar. If you see the printed message in the Eclipse console, you know everything is working properly. If you want advanced features like Spring tooling or Maven integration, you can open **Help > Eclipse Marketplace** and search for these plugins. Installing them adds direct support for backend frameworks and build tools. You can then do all your coding, refactoring, debugging, and testing inside Eclipse without leaving this environment.

Managing Dependencies with Maven

You can manage project dependencies efficiently by using Maven, a popular build automation tool in the Java ecosystem. You can think of Maven as a tool that helps define project structure, handle external libraries, run builds, and streamline collaboration. You can express project details and dependencies in a central file, often named **pom.xml**. You do not need to manually download JAR files or fiddle with classpaths. You add a dependency entry to **pom.xml**, and Maven fetches it from a remote repository. You can rely on Maven's standard project layout, which organizes code into recognizable directories for sources, tests, and resources. You can also run tests, package applications, generate documentation, and integrate directly with IDEs and continuous integration systems. You can consider Maven the stepping stone toward cleaner builds, easier transitions between developers, and simpler integration of libraries that enhance backend development.

You can begin installing Maven by visiting the official Apache Maven website at *https://maven.apache.org/download.cgi* and locating a stable binary release. You can download the binary tar.gz file to your system. For instance, you can run:

```
wget https://downloads.apache.org/maven/maven-
3/3.9.3/binaries/apache-maven-3.9.3-bin.tar.gz
```

(adjusting the version if a newer release is available). After downloading, you can extract the archive:

```
tar -xvf apache-maven-3.9.3-bin.tar.gz
```

This step creates a directory such as **apache-maven-3.9.3**. You can move this directory to a system-wide location, for example:

```
sudo mv apache-maven-3.9.3 /usr/local/maven
```

Then, you can add Maven's **bin** directory to your PATH by editing **~/.bashrc**:

```
export M2_HOME=/usr/local/maven
export PATH=$M2_HOME/bin:$PATH
```

After saving and running **source ~/.bashrc**, you can verify Maven by typing:

```
mvn -v
```

You should see Maven's version and Java details printed to the terminal. Next, you create a simple project using Maven's built-in **archetypes**. You can easily navigate to a development directory and run a command to generate a new project skeleton:

```
mvn archetype:generate -DgroupId=com.gitforgits -
DartifactId=backend-app -DarchetypeArtifactId=maven-archetype-
quickstart -DinteractiveMode=false
```

This above command creates a directory named **backend-app** containing a standard project layout. You can **cd backend-app** and see a **pom.xml** file at the root. By listing files inside **src/main/java**, you can find a Java source file, and **src/test/java** contains a test. This layout aligns with Maven conventions, letting you place application code in **src/main/java** and test code in **src/test/java**. You can run **mvn clean package** to compile the code and create a packaged artifact, typically a JAR file stored in **target/**.

You can also add dependencies to **pom.xml** by editing that file with a text editor. For instance, if you want to add JUnit 5 for testing, you can add a **<dependency>** element inside the **<dependencies>** section:

```
<dependencies>
    <dependency>
        <groupId>org.junit.jupiter</groupId>
        <artifactId>junit-jupiter-api</artifactId>
```

```
            <version>5.9.2</version>
            <scope>test</scope>
        </dependency>
    </dependencies>
```

You can save **pom.xml** and run **mvn test**. Maven downloads JUnit automatically and runs tests. If you omit the dependency, you would need to manually handle the JAR files. Maven eliminates that step, freeing you to focus on coding. This approach extends to any library. If your backend requires JSON processing, you can add dependencies for Jackson or Gson by specifying their coordinates (groupId, artifactId, version). Maven then fetches them and includes them in the classpath during builds and execution phases. You can rely on version numbers to manage updates. If you need a newer library version, you just adjust the **<version>** tag and rerun

```
mvn clean compile
```

or

```
mvn dependency:resolve
```

Later, you can integrate Maven with Eclipse to streamline development further. Since you already installed Eclipse, you can use the "Maven Integration" plugin if not already included. You can open Eclipse and choose **Help > Eclipse Marketplace**. You can search for "Maven Integration for Eclipse" or if using the Eclipse for Java Developers package, Maven support might be built-in. Once Maven support is active in Eclipse, you can import your project by clicking **File > Import > Existing Maven Projects**. You can select **backend-app** or any Maven-based project directory, and Eclipse recognizes **pom.xml**, sets up the classpath, and provides code completion and navigation features. You can run code or tests directly from Eclipse, and any new dependency you add to **pom.xml** is automatically resolved when you update the project (**Right-click project > Maven > Update Project**).

You can run a few more commands to get comfortable with Maven. For example, **mvn dependency:tree** shows all dependencies and their versions, helping you understand what libraries are included indirectly. If you face conflicts, Maven's dependency tree helps identify which transitive dependencies cause issues. You can also run **mvn dependency:purge-local-repository** to clear cached dependencies and force Maven to re-download them, which is helpful if something corrupts the local repository. Another handy command, **mvn clean install**, compiles, tests, and installs the project artifact to the local repository (**~/.m2/repository**), making it available to other local Maven projects. If you have multiple projects that depend on each other, installing them locally allows easy integration without manual copying of files.

You can also incorporate plugins into Maven. For instance, you can use the **maven-compiler-plugin** to set the Java version or the **maven-surefire-plugin** to run tests. These plugins are defined in **pom.xml** under **<build><plugins>** and require a **<configuration>** section to specify their behavior. If you want to enforce Java 17 compilation, you can include something like:

```
<plugin>
  <groupId>org.apache.maven.plugins</groupId>
  <artifactId>maven-compiler-plugin</artifactId>
  <version>3.10.1</version>
  <configuration>
    <source>17</source>
    <target>17</target>
  </configuration>
</plugin>
```

After adding this, **mvn compile** always compiles code with Java 17 compliance. As you incorporate frameworks like Spring Boot, you can add the Spring Boot Maven plugin to handle packaging the application as an executable JAR. Running a single **mvn spring-boot:run** command can start the backend application, benefiting from all dependencies defined in **pom.xml**.

You can continuously refine your **pom.xml** as the project evolves. Adding dependencies for logging frameworks like Logback or Log4j, testing libraries like Mockito, or tools like Flyway for database migrations follows the same pattern. You add a **<dependency>** entry, specify the right version, run a build command, and the libraries integrate seamlessly. By using Maven, you maintain a single source of truth about your application's dependencies. If teammates join the project, they just pull the source code and run **mvn compile** to get a working environment. If you later switch machines or set up build agents on a CI server, the same commands produce identical results. This consistency simplifies troubleshooting and ensures predictable builds at every stage of the backend's lifecycle.

Project Structure and Version Control

Say you've got a Maven project with a standard layout. It's a good idea to take another look at that layout and understand why it's important for backend development. You previously created a project named **backend-app** using Maven's archetype command. Inside the **backend-app**, you have a **pom.xml** file at the root that defines project metadata, dependencies, and plugins. Under **src/main/java**, you have all your main source code. This folder holds packages corresponding to your application's domain and logic. Under **src/main/resources**, you can store configuration files, resource bundles, or templates that your code might load at runtime. For testing, you have **src/test/java**, which mirrors the structure of **src/main/java** but for test classes, and **src/test/resources** for test-related configuration. When you package your application, Maven collects compiled classes and resources into **target/**, which becomes the staging area for building JAR files or other artifacts. By following these conventions, you produce a consistent layout that other developers recognize easily. This structure benefits you when integrating IDEs, build pipelines, and frameworks that assume standard Maven project layouts.

You should integrate a version control system so you can track changes, collaborate with others, and maintain a history of your application's progress. Git is a popular distributed version control system that developers use widely. You can use Git to record snapshots of your code over time, branch off for experiments, merge features back into the main line, and revert to older versions if something breaks. To install Git on a Linux system, you can run:

```
sudo apt update
sudo apt install git
```

After installation, you can run:

```
git --version
```

to confirm that Git is properly installed. You can then configure your Git identity by setting your name and email address, so commits are associated with you. You can run:

```
git config --global user.name "Your Name"
git config --global user.email "you@gitforgits.com"
```

Replace "Your Name" and the email address with your actual details. The **--global** flag ensures that these settings apply system-wide for all your projects. You can also configure other preferences, such as using a preferred editor for commit messages:

```
git config --global core.editor nano
```

This example sets **nano** as the default editor, but you can pick vim or any other text editor you prefer. You can then initialize a Git repository in your **backend-app** project directory. By navigating into the directory and running:

```
cd backend-app
git init
```

you create a **.git** folder that tracks versions. You can check the status with **git status**, which shows that no files are staged yet. Since this is a Maven project, you likely do not want to include build artifacts or IDE-specific files in version control. To handle this, you can create a **.gitignore** file at the root of the project to specify patterns that Git should ignore. For a Maven project, a typical **.gitignore** might include:

```
target/
*.log
*.class
.idea/
*.iml
.settings/
```

You can create and edit this file:

```
nano .gitignore
```

Add the lines mentioned above, then save and exit. With **.gitignore** in place, Git no longer suggests adding these ignored files. You can run **git status** again to see what files remain. Usually, your **pom.xml**, **src/main/java**, **src/main/resources**, and any code files remain visible.

You can add all these untracked files to the staging area with:

```
git add .
```

This command stages everything except those ignored by **.gitignore**. You can then commit the staged changes with:

```
git commit -m "Initial commit of backend-app project
structure"
```

This creates a first commit that records your project structure. If you run **git log**, you see a history containing only this initial commit. Over time, as you add code, modify files, or integrate dependencies, you run similar commands: **git add <file>** and **git commit -m "<message>"**. Each commit forms part of a timeline of changes, allowing you to travel back in history and see previous states of your code. This practice helps when diagnosing issues or understanding how certain files evolved.

You can create branches to isolate features or experiments. For example, if you want to work on a new feature without affecting the main code line, you can run:

```
git branch feature-xyz
git checkout feature-xyz
```

This creates and switches to the **`feature-xyz`** branch. Changes you commit now only appear in that branch. When you are satisfied, you can merge them back into the main branch by checking out the main branch and running:

```
git checkout main
git merge feature-xyz
```

If no conflicts arise, the merge adds all changes from **`feature-xyz`** to **`main`**. If conflicts do appear, Git highlights them in the affected files, and you can edit to resolve differences.

You can also integrate Git with remote repositories, such as ones hosted on GitHub, GitLab, or Bitbucket. By creating a new repository on a remote hosting service and copying its remote URL, you can link your local project to that remote:

```
git remote add origin https://github.com/yourusername/backend-app.git
```

This command associates **`origin`** with the remote repository's URL. After this, you can **`git push -u origin main`** to upload your local commits to GitHub. Team members or collaborators can clone this repository and work together. Each contributor commits locally and pushes changes to the remote. By pulling updates **`git pull origin main`**, everyone stays synchronized.

Next, if you integrate Eclipse with Git, you can use built-in source control tools within the IDE. Eclipse includes a perspective called "Git" that helps visualize branches, commits, and changes. To import your already Git-initialized project into Eclipse, you can open **`File > Import > Existing Maven Projects`**, point to the **`backend-app`** directory, and Eclipse will detect the **`pom.xml`** and create a project. The Git perspective (**`Window > Perspective > Open Perspective > Other > Git`**) helps you review commits, diffs, and branches without leaving the IDE. You can commit and push changes directly from Eclipse's interface if that suits your workflow. This integration lets you manage version control and code development in one place.

Summary

So, here's a quick review of the main things we've learned in this chapter: first, you installed and set up the JDK, and then you used Eclipse with the IDE and managed the project dependencies using Maven. You created a standard Maven project structure that separated the main source code, resources, and test files, making sure everyone knew where to place classes and configuration. You also integrated Maven's project object model to specify dependencies, which made it possible to fetch libraries automatically from remote repositories. You also did steps to build packages and run tests with Maven commands, which got you a workflow that reduced manual efforts.

Then, you set up version control with Git, which makes it easier to record incremental changes and keep track of modifications over time. You also created a repository, defined ignore patterns for build artifacts, and produced a stable environment where branches allowed parallel development. You used commits to capture consistent states and set up a foundation for collaboration. You connected all these elements to create a workspace that can scale, which makes it easier to onboard others and handle increasing complexity.

CHAPTER 3: INTRODUCTION TO SPRING AND SPRING BOOT

Up and Running with Spring

The Spring framework makes backend development a breeze. It's got a huge ecosystem of modules and features that you can use. It's pretty popular in the Java world since it makes enterprise apps less complex. It's a set of tools that brought in concepts like dependency injection, which lets you define how components interact without hardcoding their relationships. With Spring, you can connect objects by describing dependencies, so you don't have to manually instantiate classes in a rigid manner. These patterns encourage cleaner code and better testability. And with Spring's layered approach to building apps, you've got this flexible framework to work with. You could break complex systems into smaller, more manageable parts and count on Spring to integrate them. You also had access to a bunch of extensions, making it easier to integrate with databases, messaging systems, and security layers. Spring's popularity is due to the fact that it supports flexible architectures, it follows the convention-over-configuration principles, and adapts to changes with minimal friction.

You can start working with Spring by including it as a dependency in your Maven project. You can open your **pom.xml** and add the appropriate coordinates. Before doing that, you should understand that Spring came as a collection of modules. At a minimum, you might consider **spring-context** and **spring-beans** to enable core dependency injection features. You can add something like:

```
<dependencies>
    <dependency>
        <groupId>org.springframework</groupId>
        <artifactId>spring-context</artifactId>
        <version>5.3.27</version>
    </dependency>
    <dependency>
        <groupId>org.springframework</groupId>
        <artifactId>spring-beans</artifactId>
        <version>5.3.27</version>
    </dependency>
</dependencies>
```

You then choose a recent stable version. After saving **pom.xml**, you run **mvn clean compile** to download these dependencies. If you prefer a more minimal setup, you could pick a single starter dependency once you introduce Spring Boot. But at this point, understanding raw

Spring installation is valuable. Once Maven finishes downloading, your classpath contains Spring libraries.

Next, you then define a configuration class as below:

```
import org.springframework.context.annotation.Bean;
import org.springframework.context.annotation.Configuration;
@Configuration
public class AppConfig {
    @Bean
    public GreetingService greetingService() {
        return new GreetingService();
    }
}
```

You can also define a **GreetingService** class:

```
public class GreetingService {
    public String greet() {
        return "Hello from Spring!";
    }
}
```

You can now write a main class that loads this configuration:

```
import org.springframework.context.ApplicationContext;
import
org.springframework.context.annotation.AnnotationConfigApplica
tionContext;
public class SpringTest {
    public static void main(String[] args) {
        ApplicationContext context = new
AnnotationConfigApplicationContext(AppConfig.class);
        GreetingService service =
context.getBean(GreetingService.class);
```

```
        System.out.println(service.greet());
    }
}
```

You can run this main method and should see the greeting printed, confirming that Spring loaded your configuration, created a **GreetingService** bean, and injected it into the application context. You did not manually instantiate **GreetingService** in your main method. You asked Spring for it. By doing so, you avoided hardcoding dependencies, enabling you to switch implementations easily if needed.

You can take this setup to the next level by adding more beans or introducing interfaces. For instance, if **GreetingService** implemented an interface **IGreetingService**, you could swap implementations simply by changing the configuration. You can create a second class **FriendlyGreetingService** that returns a different message and update your **AppConfig** to return that bean instead. Running the code again would produce a different greeting without changing the main logic. This demonstrates Spring's flexibility in managing components.

You can also integrate Spring with other libraries. For accessing property files, you can add **spring-core** and use **@PropertySource** annotations, or for database access, you can add **spring-jdbc** and define data sources. Each addition requires updating **pom.xml** and re-running **mvn compile**. Spring's ecosystem is all about a modular approach. You can only add the things you need, which reduces unnecessary complexity. And later on, when you move to Spring Boot, things get even easier because Boot packages start dependencies that bundle common modules together. But knowing the raw Spring setup helps you understand what Spring Boot does for you.

So now, you've got a working Java project, handled by Maven, developed in Eclipse, version-controlled by Git, and integrated with Spring dependencies. You created configuration classes, defined beans, and tested object retrieval through Spring's application context. This is just a stepping stone. Next, you can add services, controllers, and repositories. For now, just know that you can wire beans together and run simple Spring-powered code, which means you've got Spring running locally. As you adopt more Spring modules, you can scale this approach. If something doesn't behave as expected, you can count on Spring's clear error messages and its extensive documentation from its official site or community resources. Just keep adding features one step at a time, and run the code to check the output of each change. You can also start thinking ahead about how Spring Boot will make your life easier. Instead of adding a bunch of dependencies and configuration classes manually, it provides a set of "starters" that include the most commonly needed modules. It'll also automate tasks like running embedded servers, scanning components, and applying sensible defaults.

You've probably noticed that getting Spring up and running involves adding dependencies, writing a configuration class, and creating beans. If you want, you can make a small library of beans and start using methods from them, organizing packages by domain. And if you add a logging framework dependency, you can log messages. And if you add JUnit and use Spring's testing support, you can write tests that load the application context and verify bean behavior. Each step builds on what you have now, constructing a layered backend that handles complexity through modular design and dependency injection.

Getting Started with Spring Boot

At this point, we've got a working Spring environment, and we've figured out how to set up beans and load an application context manually. There's a way to make the whole process easier and cut down on all the extra steps by using Spring Boot. The main idea behind Spring Boot is to make bootstrapping, configuration, and starting servers easier so we can focus on writing application logic instead of dealing with low-level setup. With Spring Boot, we add a single starter dependency, and the framework automatically configures components, selects defaults, and wires up common services, which lets us get an application running quickly. Instead of dealing with XML configurations or writing multiple annotation-based config classes for basic tasks, it'll infer defaults and give us embedded servers like Tomcat, so we can run a web app with a single command.

A practical way to start involves adding the Spring Boot starter dependencies to our existing Maven project. We can open the **pom.xml** file and include something like:

```
<dependencies>
    <dependency>
        <groupId>org.springframework.boot</groupId>
        <artifactId>spring-boot-starter</artifactId>
        <version>3.1.2</version>
    </dependency>

    <dependency>
        <groupId>org.springframework.boot</groupId>
        <artifactId>spring-boot-starter-test</artifactId>
        <scope>test</scope>
        <version>3.1.2</version>
    </dependency>
```

```
</dependencies>
<build>
    <plugins>
        <plugin>
            <groupId>org.springframework.boot</groupId>
            <artifactId>spring-boot-maven-plugin</artifactId>
            <version>3.1.2</version>
        </plugin>
    </plugins>
</build>
```

By saving these changes and running **mvn clean package**, Maven fetches Spring Boot and related components. Another approach is to visit the Spring Initializr website at *https://start.spring.io/*, which provides a web interface to create a starter project. Since we already have a project, manually adding dependencies is enough. The chosen versions can match current stable releases. Once this is done, the classpath now includes Spring Boot starters.

From this point, now we create an entry point for the application that involves a single class annotated with **@SpringBootApplication**. For instance, let us consider a file named **AppMain.java**:

```
import org.springframework.boot.SpringApplication;
import
org.springframework.boot.autoconfigure.SpringBootApplication;
@SpringBootApplication
public class AppMain {
    public static void main(String[] args) {
        SpringApplication.run(AppMain.class, args);
    }
}
```

By annotating with **@SpringBootApplication**, Spring Boot scans the package of **AppMain** and sub-packages for Spring components like **@Configuration**, **@Controller**, **@Service**, and **@Repository** annotated classes. It applies auto-configuration logic for common scenarios. For example, if we add **spring-boot-starter-**

web as a dependency, Boot auto-configures a web environment with an embedded Tomcat server, sets up dispatcher servlets, and configures default settings, so we can immediately start defining REST endpoints without manual server configuration. If we only have **spring-boot-starter**, Boot still applies core configurations and sets up basic application contexts.

If the goal is to quickly spin up a web backend, we can add another starter dependency for the web environment:

```
<dependency>
    <groupId>org.springframework.boot</groupId>
    <artifactId>spring-boot-starter-web</artifactId>
    <version>3.1.2</version>
</dependency>
```

Rerunning **mvn compile** ensures these libraries are downloaded. After this, by running **mvn spring-boot:run**, the application starts, and an embedded server listens on **http://localhost:8080** by default. Without writing any server configuration code, we have a web server ready. To confirm everything works, define a simple REST controller class:

```
import org.springframework.web.bind.annotation.GetMapping;
import org.springframework.web.bind.annotation.RestController;
@RestController
public class HelloController {
    @GetMapping("/hello")
    public String hello() {
        return "Hello from Spring Boot!";
    }
}
```

After saving this class in the same package as **AppMain** or a sub-package, rerun **mvn spring-boot:run** or run the **AppMain** main method directly from Eclipse. Once the application starts, open a browser or use **curl** to visit **http://localhost:8080/hello**. The response should be "Hello from Spring Boot!", proving that auto-configuration set up a web server, mapped **/hello** to this controller, and wired everything together.

Starter dependencies represent one of the biggest time-savers in Spring Boot. Instead of individually adding **spring-context**, **spring-web**, **spring-webmvc**, **jackson-**

databind, or other libraries, the **spring-boot-starter-web** dependency pulls in everything needed for web development. This reduces the complexity of choosing and managing dozens of libraries. Similarly, if the application requires JDBC integration or JPA, adding **spring-boot-starter-jdbc** or **spring-boot-starter-data-jmasguppa** fetches the required libraries and configures data sources, transaction managers, and entity managers automatically when the required drivers or configurations are detected.

Auto-configuration is an important idea. Spring Boot checks the classpath and beans to apply configurations based on certain conditions. For example, if **spring-web** is present, Boot sets up a **DispatcherServlet** automatically. If a **DataSource** is present and **spring-boot-starter-data-jpa** is on the classpath, Boot configures **EntityManagerFactory**, **TransactionManager**, and other JPA-related beans. If **Thymeleaf** is included, Boot configures template resolvers. By relying on classpath presence and environment properties, Boot decides what to configure, freeing us from repetitive code.

To see auto-configuration in action, we can add a database driver and the **spring-boot-starter-data-jpa** dependency.

For instance:

```
<dependency>
    <groupId>org.springframework.boot</groupId>
    <artifactId>spring-boot-starter-data-jpa</artifactId>
    <version>3.1.2</version>
</dependency>
<dependency>
    <groupId>org.postgresql</groupId>
    <artifactId>postgresql</artifactId>
    <version>42.6.0</version>
</dependency>
```

After adding these and running the application again, Boot notices a database driver and JPA starter. If a **application.properties** file in **src/main/resources** includes something like:

```
spring.datasource.url=jdbc:postgresql://localhost:5432/mydb
spring.datasource.username=myuser
spring.datasource.password=mypass
```

```
spring.jpa.hibernate.ddl-auto=update
```

Boot configures a **DataSource** and JPA's **EntityManager** automatically. Without writing a single line of configuration code, we get a fully operational JPA environment, ready to define entities and repositories. Creating a simple entity and repository:

```
import jakarta.persistence.Entity;
import jakarta.persistence.Id;
@Entity
public class Book {
    @Id
    private Long id;
    private String title;
    // Getters and setters omitted for brevity
}
import org.springframework.data.jpa.repository.JpaRepository;
public interface BookRepository extends JpaRepository<Book,
Long> {
}
```

Once these classes are in place, Boot automatically creates an implementation of **BookRepository** and connects it to the database. We can then inject this repository into controllers or services and start performing CRUD operations. No manual bean definitions required. This demonstrates how starter dependencies and auto-configuration combine to accelerate development.

Another helpful feature is the Actuator, which provides endpoints to monitor and manage the application. By adding:

```
<dependency>
    <groupId>org.springframework.boot</groupId>
    <artifactId>spring-boot-starter-actuator</artifactId>
    <version>3.1.2</version>
</dependency>
```

Boot auto-configures health checks and other endpoints available at **/actuator** routes by default. We can explore metrics, health status, and environment details. By leveraging these starters, we avoid writing large amounts of infrastructure code. The application grows faster, and we focus on domain logic rather than boilerplate.

Configuration can be adjusted if defaults are not desirable. Instead of relying on the default **8080** port, adding **server.port=9090** to **application.properties** changes it. Instead of using in-memory databases, providing the above-mentioned JDBC URL points to a real database. Instead of default logging, adding logback configurations or environment variables customizes logging. The auto-configuration and starters handle the heavy lifting, but developers remain free to override defaults in **application.properties** or **application.yml**.

Debugging auto-configuration is straightforward if something doesn't behave as expected. Running the application with **--debug** flag (**mvn spring-boot:run -Dspring-boot.run.arguments=--debug**) prints diagnostic information about why certain beans were or were not configured. This helps understand Boot's decision process. Another option is using **@ConditionalOn...** annotations inside custom configurations if advanced scenarios arise, though beginners usually find the defaults good enough.

Spring Boot also integrates smoothly with testing frameworks. The **spring-boot-starter-test** dependency includes JUnit, Mockito, and specialized test runners. Annotating tests with **@SpringBootTest** loads a full application context for integration tests, while **@WebMvcTest** can load a partial context focused on controller tests. Just like with the runtime configuration, test configurations use auto-configuration to simplify testing. A single **mvn test** command runs all these tests easily, relying on Boot to supply a consistent, known environment.

As the application matures, adding more starters aligns it with additional features. Messaging support (e.g., RabbitMQ) or caching (e.g., Redis) can be integrated by adding respective starters. Boot then sets up the required beans. Even building docker images for deployment is easier with Boot's build plugins. Without changing code, **mvn spring-boot:build-image** creates a container image ready to run in a production environment, all guided by conventional defaults.

By adopting Spring Boot, we essentially embraced convention-over-configuration principles. The original Spring offered powerful features, but required explicit setup and configuration classes. Boot builds on top of that foundation, guessing intentions from what's on the classpath and simplifying the developer experience. The difference is substantial: what once took multiple steps, extensive configuration classes, and reading many reference documents can often be accomplished by adding the right starter dependency and a few lines in **application.properties**.

At this stage, we have a running Spring Boot application with minimal code. We can keep building upon it by adding controllers, services, repositories, and domain objects. The application can grow from a simple "hello world" endpoint to a fully-fledged backend service, integrated with databases, messaging systems, authentication providers, and more. Boot will continue to handle tedious details behind the scenes, allowing us to remain productive and focused on solving business problems.

Dependency Injection and Inversion of Control

Dependency injection and inversion of control are all about keeping components from being too dependent on each other. This makes it so systems can smoothly adapt over time. With these, classes don't have to create or manage their dependencies directly; a container (Spring's ApplicationContext) takes care of that at runtime by wiring objects together. Instead of manually creating objects, code requests them from the container. This makes systems more flexible. If you change a component's dependencies or swap implementations, you don't have to rework big chunks of code. With DI, objects declare their dependencies through constructors or properties, and the IoC container (Spring) automatically injects them. The end result is a codebase where you can adjust behavior by changing configuration or bean definitions, rather than rewriting logic.

It's helpful to see a practical example. Let's say we've got a service layer that depends on a data-access component. To start, let's define an interface for data access as below:

```
public interface BookDataSource {
    String findBookTitleById(Long id);
}
```

Then provide an implementation as shown below:

```
import org.springframework.stereotype.Component;
@Component
public class InMemoryBookDataSource implements BookDataSource
{
    @Override
    public String findBookTitleById(Long id) {
        // For demonstration, return a dummy title
        return "Spring Boot in Action";
    }
}
```

Note the **@Component** annotation, which tells Spring to treat this class as a bean candidate. Since we have a Spring Boot application with component scanning, this class is discovered at runtime.

Next, create a service class that depends on **BookDataSource**:

```
import org.springframework.stereotype.Service;
@Service
public class BookService {
    private final BookDataSource dataSource;
    public BookService(BookDataSource dataSource) {
        this.dataSource = dataSource;
    }
    public String getBookTitle(Long id) {
        return dataSource.findBookTitleById(id);
    }
}
```

In the above program, **BookService** receives **BookDataSource** via its constructor. Spring looks at the available beans that implement **BookDataSource** and injects the **InMemoryBookDataSource** bean automatically. No code in **BookService** references **InMemoryBookDataSource** directly, reducing coupling. If we create another implementation and mark it with **@Component**, then by changing a configuration, we could pick that implementation at runtime without modifying **BookService**'s code.

To test or run this, add a simple controller that uses **BookService**:

```
import org.springframework.web.bind.annotation.GetMapping;
import org.springframework.web.bind.annotation.RestController;
@RestController
public class BookController {
    private final BookService bookService;

    public BookController(BookService bookService) {
        this.bookService = bookService;
    }
    @GetMapping("/book")
```

```
    public String getBook() {
        return bookService.getBookTitle(1L);
    }
}
```

When the application runs, Spring creates **InMemoryBookDataSource**, **BookService**, and **BookController** beans. It wires them together by injecting **BookService** into **BookController** and **BookDataSource** into **BookService**. By hitting **http://localhost:8080/book**, the response displays "Spring Boot in Action." If we want to return different titles or load data from a database, change the **BookDataSource** implementation. No adjustments in **BookService** or **BookController** are needed.

If testing is required, create a test that uses **@SpringBootTest** and injects **BookService**. Mocking the data source becomes easy if a mocking library like Mockito is introduced. Instead of rewriting logic, modify bean definitions to supply a mock bean. For example:

```
import org.junit.jupiter.api.Test;
import org.springframework.boot.test.context.SpringBootTest;
import org.springframework.boot.test.mock.mockito.MockBean;
import static org.mockito.Mockito.*;
@SpringBootTest
public class BookServiceTest {
    @MockBean
    private BookDataSource dataSource;
    @Test
    public void testGetBookTitle() {

when(dataSource.findBookTitleById(1L)).thenReturn("Mocked
Title");
        // At runtime, BookService uses the mocked dataSource
bean.
        // Verify logic without changing BookService source
code.
    }
```

```
}
```

By using DI and IoC, dev teams can change code quickly, add fake dependencies easily, and change behavior by tweaking beans and configurations rather than rewriting classes.

Creating GitforGits Base Application

With DI, IoC, and Spring Boot in place, it's time to start the GitforGits project, a sample book publishing application that demonstrates practical backend concepts. We here begin by initializing a new Spring Boot application or adapting the one created earlier. If starting fresh, the Spring Initializr at *https://start.spring.io/* can generate a new project. Choose "Maven Project," "Java," a recent Spring Boot version, and then add dependencies like "Spring Web," "Spring Data JPA," "H2 Database" (for quick demos), and "Spring Boot DevTools." Download the generated zip, extract it, and open it in Eclipse. If continuing from the current codebase, just add these dependencies to **pom.xml**.

Once dependencies are ready, a main class **GitforGitsApplication.java** should look like this:

```
import org.springframework.boot.SpringApplication;
import
org.springframework.boot.autoconfigure.SpringBootApplication;
@SpringBootApplication
public class GitforGitsApplication {
    public static void main(String[] args) {
        SpringApplication.run(GitforGitsApplication.class,
args);
    }
}
```

By annotating with **@SpringBootApplication**, the project auto-configures components and scans for beans in the current package and sub-packages. Now here, you create a package structure to keep code organized as below:

- **com.gitforgits** as the base package.
- **com.gitforgits.config** for configuration classes.
- **com.gitforgits.model** for entity classes.

- **com.gitforgits.repository** for data access interfaces.
- **com.gitforgits.service** for business logic.
- **com.gitforgits.web** for controllers.

Next, create an entity class to represent a book being published:

```
package com.gitforgits.model;
import jakarta.persistence.Entity;
import jakarta.persistence.Id;
@Entity
public class Book {
    @Id
    private Long id;
    private String title;
    private String author;
    private String description;
    // getters and setters omitted for brevity
}
```

This entity maps to a table named **Book**. Spring Boot, with **spring-boot-starter-data-jpa** and **spring-boot-starter-h2**, automatically configures an in-memory H2 database. On application startup, an in-memory schema is created.

We then add a repository interface:

```
package com.gitforgits.repository;
import org.springframework.data.jpa.repository.JpaRepository;
import com.gitforgits.model.Book;
public interface BookRepository extends JpaRepository<Book,
Long> {
}
```

This repository lets us perform CRUD operations on **Book** without writing queries. Spring Boot creates an implementation at runtime.

Next, create a service that depends on **BookRepository**:

```
package com.gitforgits.service;
import org.springframework.stereotype.Service;
import com.gitforgits.repository.BookRepository;
import com.gitforgits.model.Book;
import java.util.Optional;
@Service
public class BookService {
    private final BookRepository repository;
    public BookService(BookRepository repository) {
        this.repository = repository;
    }
    public Optional<Book> getBook(Long id) {
        return repository.findById(id);
    }
    public Book saveBook(Book book) {
        return repository.save(book);
    }
}
```

This service here uses DI to receive a **BookRepository** instance. We did not instantiate **BookRepository** manually. Spring does it automatically.

And now finally, create a controller to expose endpoints:

```
package com.gitforgits.web;
import org.springframework.web.bind.annotation.*;
import com.gitforgits.service.BookService;
import com.gitforgits.model.Book;
import java.util.Optional;
@RestController
@RequestMapping("/api/books")
```

```java
public class BookController {
    private final BookService service;
    public BookController(BookService service) {
        this.service = service;
    }
    @GetMapping("/{id}")
    public Optional<Book> getBookById(@PathVariable Long id) {
        return service.getBook(id);
    }
    @PostMapping
    public Book createBook(@RequestBody Book book) {
        return service.saveBook(book);
    }
}
```

This **BookController** listens at **/api/books**. The GET request to **http://localhost:8080/api/books/1** attempts to retrieve a book with ID 1. And the POST request with a JSON body to **/api/books** creates a new book record in the in-memory database. By default, the H2 console can be accessed at **http://localhost:8080/h2-console** if **spring.h2.console.enabled=true** is set in **application.properties**. The console allows inspecting the **Book** table and verifying that data is persisted in memory.

Because IoC and DI drive object creation and wiring, no class instantiates **BookRepository** or **BookService** directly. If later we decide to store books in a different data source or add caching, no changes to **BookController** logic are needed. Just replace the repository bean or add a caching layer in the service. This architecture ensures each layer focuses on its job: controllers handle HTTP requests and responses, services implement business logic, repositories manage data operations. Each layer depends on abstractions (interfaces) rather than concrete implementations, enabling flexibility. If we decide to introduce a different data source or a remote API for fetching books, we could implement a new repository class that uses REST calls or another technology. After adjusting bean definitions, **BookService** would receive that new repository without altering its code. Similarly, if we add a second entity, like **Author**, we create an **Author** entity, **AuthorRepository**, **AuthorService**, and **AuthorController** following the same pattern, scaling the application in a consistent manner.

In addition, the Spring Boot's DevTools dependency aids in development by automatically restarting the application on code changes. The addition of **`spring-boot-devtools`** in **`pom.xml`** enables hot swapping in many cases. If we edit **`BookController`** and save it, it might trigger a quick restart for fast iteration. By testing endpoints often, we make sure that DI and IoC principles keep code flexible, maintainable, and easy to evolve.

Summary

Overall, you got to grips with the Spring framework and how it can help build modular backend applications. You used dependency injection and inversion of control, which let components be wired together by a container instead of being hardcoded at construction. You saw how this approach made changing data sources or business logic simpler since services depended on interfaces rather than specific implementations. You also set up a basic app that automatically found beans, created contexts, and launched embedded servers.

You also got the ball rolling on the GitforGits project, kicking things off with a basic framework encompassing entities, repositories, services, and controllers. You used Spring Data JPA to access databases without having to write SQL. You tested endpoints that read and write data from memory. And you'd combined Spring Boot starters and auto-configuration with dependency injection patterns to make a flexible, easy-to-maintain foundation for the project.

CHAPTER 4: BUILDING RESTFUL APIS WITH SPRING BOOT

Understanding RESTful Web Services

These days, a lot of web apps rely on sending data and commands over the internet, and RESTful web services are a popular way to do that. REST (Representational State Transfer) works with HTTP's stateless nature, using standard methods like GET, POST, PUT, and DELETE to interact with resources identified by URLs. Instead of thinking of servers as places that run random code, REST encourages treating the server as a place where you can store resources that can be created, retrieved, updated, or deleted. Clients and servers stay separate, which makes scaling, maintaining, and evolving the system simpler. With REST, requests include representations of resources, often in JSON or XML format, and responses reflect the current state of those resources or confirm changes.

This architecture was important because it fit well with how the web worked. Instead of using complicated protocols or message formats, REST relied on more familiar conventions. Clients could navigate resources through hyperlinks, similar to how web users browse hyperlinks in HTML pages. Since each request carried enough context, servers could handle requests independently, which is called "statelessness." This approach made caching, load balancing, and distribution across multiple servers better. If a certain resource got a lot of requests, caching responses reduced the load. If there's a surge in traffic, adding more servers to handle the same requests becomes easier, since no server needs to store session-specific data. The interface was defined by HTTP methods and status codes, so developers could understand an API's behavior without reading lengthy specifications. GET fetches resources, POST creates new instances, PUT updates existing ones, and DELETE removes resources. Having standard responses and formats made it easier for different teams, clients, and technologies to work together.

REST also had an impact on development styles. Instead of building tightly coupled backends and frontends, teams created reusable APIs that supported various clients—web, mobile, IoT, or third-party integrations. For example, a smartphone app could use the same REST endpoints as a web frontend, which reduces duplication and allows for more flexible architectures. Third-party developers or partners could integrate by calling documented endpoints. The application's logic and data were tucked behind these endpoints, and as requirements changed, teams could tweak endpoints or create new ones without breaking existing clients, as long as backward compatibility was taken care of. RESTful services often returned responses in JSON, which is lightweight, easy to parse, and widely supported. JSON made it easy to integrate with JavaScript frameworks, mobile apps, or other languages.

The simplicity and standardization that REST introduced also influenced testing and debugging. Since HTTP requests were easy for humans to read and could be easily simulated with tools like curl or Postman, it was a lot easier to figure out what was going wrong. A developer could send a GET request to a resource endpoint and check the returned payload to confirm that the API behaved as expected. It also made logging requests and responses or adding monitoring tools way easier. The stateless model also helped distribute workloads across multiple nodes in a cluster. If one server goes down, the others can still handle new requests without losing user sessions or needing failover logic.

This architectural style supported a variety of backend frameworks and languages. Since REST relied on HTTP, any platform that could serve HTTP requests could implement a RESTful API. Java developers adopted frameworks like Spring Boot to quickly define endpoints by annotating controller classes and methods. Behind the scenes, Spring mapped these annotations to HTTP requests and automatically serialized Java objects into JSON for responses. The uniform interface of REST worked seamlessly with Spring's features. With minimal configuration, returning a Java object from a controller method yielded a JSON representation to the client. Interoperability and tool support became abundant, and testing frameworks, API documentation generators, and client code generators emerged, accelerating development even further.

A well-designed REST API considered resource modeling carefully. Instead of thinking in terms of verbs or actions, developers identified the nouns (resources) that represented the domain's entities. For GitforGits, these might be "books," "authors," "publishers," or "reviews." Each resource had a base endpoint, and actions translated naturally into HTTP operations. Retrieving a book used GET **`/api/books/{id}`**, creating a book used POST **`/api/books`**, updating with PUT or PATCH, and deleting with DELETE. This consistency made it easy to guess endpoints or behavior after understanding a few patterns. Also, returning proper HTTP status codes (200 OK, 201 Created, 404 Not Found, 400 Bad Request, 500 Internal Server Error) conveyed success, errors, or exceptional conditions without inventing a proprietary mechanism.

Implementing RESTful web services in Spring Boot took advantage of starter dependencies and conventions we already learned. By using **`@RestController`** and **`@RequestMapping`** annotations, endpoints are defined succinctly. For example:

```
@RestController
@RequestMapping("/api/books")
public class BookController {
    private final BookService service;
    public BookController(BookService service) {
        this.service = service;
    }
    @GetMapping("/{id}")
    public ResponseEntity<Book> getBook(@PathVariable Long id)
{
        return service.getBook(id)
                .map(book -> ResponseEntity.ok(book))
                .orElse(ResponseEntity.notFound().build());
```

```
    }
    @PostMapping
    public ResponseEntity<Book> createBook(@RequestBody Book
book) {
        Book saved = service.saveBook(book);
        return
ResponseEntity.status(HttpStatus.CREATED).body(saved);
    }
}
```

In the above sample code, the **@RestController** and **@RequestMapping** defined a base path for the resource (**/api/books**). The **@GetMapping** and **@PostMapping** annotated methods aligned with GET and POST HTTP operations. Returning **ResponseEntity** allowed controlling the status code and headers. If a book was found, **ok()** returned 200 with the book data as JSON. If not, **notFound()** returned 404. When creating a book, **status(HttpStatus.CREATED)** indicated 201. This alignment with HTTP verbs and status codes followed REST principles and made the API predictable.

The clients interacting with these endpoints make requests using standard HTTP libraries. A frontend application could call **/api/books/1** with a GET request and receive a book object in JSON. A mobile app could POST a new book by sending JSON to **/api/books** and receiving a newly created resource. Another service could integrate seamlessly without caring about the implementation details behind the endpoint. The resource representations remained stable as long as no breaking changes were introduced in the JSON structure or endpoint paths. If changes were needed, versioning endpoints or adding new fields while keeping old ones supported backward compatibility.

The REST encourages developers to think carefully about URIs and resource boundaries. Instead of forcing actions into endpoints, building a resource-oriented model improved the conceptual clarity of the API. For actions that did not fit neatly into standard CRUD operations, many developers introduced relationships or conceptual resources. Instead of **/api/books/updateTitle**, the title would be changed by sending a PUT request with a modified representation of the book to **/api/books/{id}**. The client replaced the entire resource representation, and the server updated the stored record. If a partial update was needed, some used PATCH. If linking authors to books was required, endpoints for **/api/books/{id}/authors** might represent relationships. By following standard patterns, future maintainers and integrators understood endpoints without reading lengthy custom documentation.

Adopting REST did not solve all challenges, but it provided a baseline that simplified many aspects of backend development. Combined with Spring Boot, building and exposing RESTful services became a matter of adding a few dependencies and annotating classes, saving developers from tedious manual configurations. The synergy between REST principles and Spring Boot's auto-configuration allowed producing stable, maintainable APIs rapidly, ready to serve a variety of clients.

Creating Controllers and Request Mapping

Understanding Controllers

When building RESTful APIs with Spring Boot, controllers become the core constructs for handling incoming HTTP requests and returning appropriate responses. Instead of scattering request handling logic throughout the codebase, controllers centralize the logic, ensuring a clean separation of concerns. By annotating classes with **@RestController**, Spring treats them as specialized components that receive and process requests. The methods inside these controllers map to specific resource paths and HTTP methods. For instance, **@GetMapping** for GET requests, **@PostMapping** for POST requests, and so forth. The controller methods often return domain objects, and Spring Boot automatically serializes them into JSON or another supported format.

Mapping URLs to Methods

To transform HTTP requests into actionable logic, controllers rely on mapping annotations that bind paths and HTTP methods to handler methods. The **@RequestMapping** annotation at the class level can define a base URL segment, while method-level annotations like **@GetMapping("/books")** refine the endpoint. The result is a clear and predictable mapping between incoming requests and code execution. If a client performs a GET request to **/api/books/1**, the corresponding method retrieves a book by its ID. If a client posts JSON data to **/api/books**, the corresponding method creates a new book record. This alignment mirrors REST principles, treating URIs as resource identifiers and HTTP methods as actions. Parameters extracted from paths, query strings, or request bodies flow naturally into controller method arguments.

Sample Program: Building a Sample Controller

Here's an easy example to illustrate these ideas — let's say you're creating a controller to manage book resources. Suppose we have a **BookService** class that handles business logic for retrieving and storing books. A controller named **BookController** might look like this:

```
import org.springframework.web.bind.annotation.*;
```

```java
import java.util.List;
@RestController
@RequestMapping("/api/books")
public class BookController {
    private final BookService service;
    public BookController(BookService service) {
        this.service = service;
    }
    @GetMapping
    public List<Book> getAllBooks() {
        return service.getAllBooks();
    }
    @GetMapping("/{id}")
    public Book getBookById(@PathVariable Long id) {
        return service.getBook(id).orElse(null);
    }
    @PostMapping
    public Book createBook(@RequestBody Book book) {
        return service.saveBook(book);
    }
}
```

In the above sample program, **`@RequestMapping("/api/books")`** sets the base path. The **`@GetMapping`** without an additional path maps to **`GET /api/books`** for listing all books. The **`@GetMapping("/{id}")`** maps to **`GET /api/books/{id}`** for fetching a single book. The **`@PostMapping`** maps to **`POST /api/books`** for creating a new book. If you follow these conventions, it'll be easy for a client to guess endpoints and methods. This makes it easy to think about resources and fits well with RESTful principles.

Handling HTTP Methods and Responses

Role of CRUD Operations

Most data-driven applications are all about the Create, Read, Update, and Delete cycle (CRUD). These four actions basically capture the essential ways clients interact with resources. For example, in a book management scenario, "Create" would mean adding a new book, "Read" would retrieve existing books, "Update" would modify an existing book's attributes, and "Delete" would remove a book. HTTP methods fit perfectly with these actions. POST is usually used to create new resources, GET retrieves data, PUT updates resources, and DELETE removes them. Following this mapping makes the API consistent and predictable. Clients know that sending a POST request to a collection endpoint creates something new, while a GET request retrieves data. This makes integration a breeze and makes it super easy to figure out how to use the API.

Implementing GET

Retrieving resources with GET requests represents the simplest interaction pattern. A GET request does not modify server state; it only fetches representations of existing data. Consider a scenario where we have a **`BookController`** and want to return all books or a specific one. As shown before, **`@GetMapping`** on the **`/api/books`** endpoint returns a list of books. If the request includes an ID segment, like **`/api/books/10`**, the controller retrieves the specified book. By returning a domain object or a list of domain objects, Spring converts the response into JSON automatically. Including error handling or returning a **`ResponseEntity`** type allows more control over status codes. For instance, if **`service.getBook(id)`** returns empty, returning **`ResponseEntity.notFound().build()`** communicates that no such resource exists. Handling null checks, optional values, or exceptions inside the controller methods ensures that responses reflect the resource state accurately.

Implementing POST

When clients send data to create new resources, POST requests come into play. A POST to **`/api/books`** might include JSON data representing a book's title, author, and other attributes. The controller method annotated with **`@PostMapping`** reads this data via **`@RequestBody`** and passes it to the service layer. The service then validates and stores the new book, returning the saved entity. By returning a **`ResponseEntity`** with **`HttpStatus.CREATED`** and possibly including a **`Location`** header pointing to the newly created resource's URI, clients receive feedback that the creation succeeded. If validation fails, the controller could return a **`400 Bad Request`** status. This mechanism encourages a clear contract: POST endpoints accept representations of new resources and create them if valid. The clients can rely on these behaviors across different resources, improving API usability and consistency.

For example:

```
@PostMapping
```

```
public ResponseEntity<Book> createBook(@RequestBody Book book)
{
    Book saved = service.saveBook(book);
    return
ResponseEntity.status(HttpStatus.CREATED).body(saved);
}
```

Implementing PUT

When you update existing resources, you're using the PUT method. A PUT request sends a full or partial representation of the resource to the server, intending to replace the existing state. Some folks like PUT for full replacements and PATCH for partial updates, but focusing on PUT first helps set a baseline.

Suppose a client wants to update a book's title. Sending a PUT request to **/api/books/10** with a JSON body containing a modified book object signals the server to replace the current version of the resource with this new one. The controller method annotated with **@PutMapping("/{id}")** fetches the existing book, updates its fields, and saves it. Returning **ResponseEntity.ok(updatedBook)** indicates success. If no book is found for that ID, returning **404 Not Found** helps the client understand the request outcome.

Take an example:

```
@PutMapping("/{id}")
public ResponseEntity<Book> updateBook(@PathVariable Long id,
@RequestBody Book updatedData) {
    return service.getBook(id)
        .map(existing -> {
            existing.setTitle(updatedData.getTitle());
            existing.setAuthor(updatedData.getAuthor());

existing.setDescription(updatedData.getDescription());
            Book saved = service.saveBook(existing);
            return ResponseEntity.ok(saved);
        })
        .orElse(ResponseEntity.notFound().build());
```

```
}
```

This pattern ensures the resource at the specified URI now reflects the new data sent by the client.

Implementing DELETE

Removing resources from the server's storage is performed with DELETE requests. Clients calling **DELETE /api/books/10** expect the server to remove the specified resource. If successful, returning **204 No Content** indicates that the operation succeeded and the resource no longer exists. If the resource did not exist, **404 Not Found** might be suitable. The controller method annotated with **@DeleteMapping("/{id}")** locates the book and, if found, deletes it. If no book matches the given ID, returning a **404 Not Found** helps the client understand the outcome. This uniformity applies across all resources, giving a standard approach for removal.

```
@DeleteMapping("/{id}")
public ResponseEntity<Void> deleteBook(@PathVariable Long id)
{
    if (service.deleteBook(id)) {
        return ResponseEntity.noContent().build();
    } else {
        return ResponseEntity.notFound().build();
    }
}
```

In the above sample code, **service.deleteBook(id)** returns true if a deletion occurred, false if no record was deleted. The controller returns a **204 No Content** or **404 Not Found** accordingly.

Handling Errors and Status Codes

HTTP methods and responses work best when meaningful status codes are chosen. A GET that finds no resource returns **404 Not Found**, a POST that creates something returns **201 Created**, and a bad request returns **400 Bad Request**. This helps clients understand not just the outcome but also how to adjust requests or handle failures. If an internal error occurs, returning **500 Internal Server Error** indicates a server-side problem. If clients send malformed data, **400 Bad Request** communicates that the request was invalid. By pairing proper status codes with JSON error messages or error structures, clients can programmatically handle different outcomes.

Spring makes it easy to set headers and status codes via **ResponseEntity**. If advanced error handling is needed, **@ControllerAdvice** classes can centralize exception-to-response mappings. This keeps controllers cleaner and error responses consistent. For instance, if a validation error arises when creating a book, throwing a custom exception and handling it in a **@ControllerAdvice** method that returns **400 Bad Request** and an error message yields a uniform error response approach.

Testing Endpoints

Developers can verify that these CRUD endpoints function properly by running the application and performing requests with tools like **curl** or Postman. For example, **curl -X GET http://localhost:8080/api/books** fetches all books, **curl -X GET http://localhost:8080/api/books/1** fetches a specific book, and **curl -X DELETE http://localhost:8080/api/books/1** attempts deletion. Checking the returned status codes, response bodies, and logs confirms that the controller logic aligns with expectations. Automated tests can also be written using **@SpringBootTest** and **TestRestTemplate** or **WebTestClient** to test endpoints programmatically.

Once basic CRUD is established, enhancements can be made. Adding pagination, sorting, filtering, or custom queries extends the API's capabilities. For example, **GET /api/books?author=John** might return books by a specific author. Query parameters can be read using **@RequestParam** in controller methods. Adding **@PatchMapping** for partial updates or different endpoints for batch operations can evolve the API further. While these features are not essential at the earliest stages, knowing that HTTP methods map nicely to different operations helps plan out future growth.

Integration with Services and Repositories

The controller layer sits between HTTP requests and the service layer, like a go-between. The service layer handles business logic, data validation, and interactions with repositories. The repository layer handles the database or data store. Keeping the controller simple and just translating HTTP requests into method calls on the service makes the code easy to maintain. The service can check input validity, enforce constraints, or orchestrate multiple repository calls. The controller's job is pretty much limited to mapping requests and responses, and formatting results. This layered approach helps keep things clean and organized, with each part responsible for a specific task. And if something changes with the database, the controller code can still function normally since it doesn't have a direct connection to the database.

Consistency and Documentation

Developers and clients benefit when the API design remains consistent. Using plural nouns for collection endpoints (e.g., **/api/books**) and singular resource paths for specific items (e.g., **/api/books/{id}**) makes sense. Consistent use of HTTP methods for CRUD operations and meaningful status codes ensures that anyone using the API understands how to interact with the system. Documenting endpoints, parameters, and response formats, or using tools like OpenAPI/Swagger to generate interactive documentation, helps consumers explore the API's capabilities. Even though no restricted words like "guide" can be used, providing references to official Spring documentation or code examples remains helpful.

Summary

To sum it all up, you learned how RESTful principles influenced API design, encouraging resource-oriented URIs and standard HTTP methods like GET, POST, PUT, and DELETE. You saw how controllers in Spring Boot worked as dedicated classes that sent incoming requests to handler methods with annotations like @GetMapping, @PostMapping, and so on. You also saw how returning domain objects lets Spring automatically convert them into JSON for clients. By following these patterns, you made sure endpoints were intuitive, consistent, and easy to integrate.

You also implemented CRUD operations, mapping Create to POST, Read to GET, Update to PUT, and Delete to DELETE. You also learned how to respond with the right HTTP status codes like 200 OK, 201 Created, or 404 Not Found, making it clear if something succeeded or failed. You also tested endpoints with tools like curl, making sure the responses matched what was expected. You also thought about how to deal with errors, using ResponseEntity and ControllerAdvice to give consistent and helpful responses when requests are invalid or resources are missing. As you went through all this, you realized that using request mappings, HTTP methods, and status codes the right way makes your backend services built on Spring Boot more reliable, clear, and scalable.

Chapter 5: Data Persistence with Hibernate ORM and JPA

Configuring Hibernate with Spring Boot

Introducing Hibernate and JPA

A lot of Java apps need to store data in a way that'll last, especially when it's always changing. Instead of writing raw SQL and dealing with JDBC code, it's better to use Hibernate ORM with the JPA. It maps Java classes to database tables, so you don't have to deal with most of the direct database handling. The JPA spec defines how entities, relationships, and queries work, and Hibernate provides a mature and robust implementation. Using entities instead of SQL strings makes for cleaner code. This approach also makes it easier to refactor, since you only have to adjust entity classes and annotations when you rename fields or change relationships. It makes data access patterns more consistent, and integrating with Spring Boot streamlines configuration. If you add the right dependencies and properties, your application will automatically get a fully functional persistence layer that can evolve alongside the domain model.

Setting up Dependencies and Configuration

Before using Hibernate and JPA, adding the required dependencies to the Maven **pom.xml** is essential. Consider starting with **spring-boot-starter-data-jpa** and a database driver. If a PostgreSQL database is preferred, then include the following:

```
<dependencies>
    <dependency>
        <groupId>org.springframework.boot</groupId>
        <artifactId>spring-boot-starter-data-jpa</artifactId>
        <version>3.1.2</version>
    </dependency>
    <dependency>
        <groupId>org.postgresql</groupId>
        <artifactId>postgresql</artifactId>
        <version>42.6.0</version>
    </dependency>
</dependencies>
```

With these in place, the application can connect to PostgreSQL and use JPA-based repositories. Specify the data source settings in **application.properties**:

```
spring.datasource.url=jdbc:postgresql://localhost:5432/gitforg
itsdb
spring.datasource.username=gitforgitsuser
spring.datasource.password=yourpassword
spring.jpa.hibernate.ddl-auto=update
spring.jpa.show-sql=true
```

The **ddl-auto** setting directs Hibernate to update the schema based on entity definitions. During this development, this saves time by automatically aligning the database schema with code changes. The **show-sql=true** property prints the generated SQL in the console, aiding understanding and debugging.

Entity Modeling with JPA Annotations

To create a domain model entity, it requires annotating a simple Java class with **@Entity**. For the GitforGits application, consider a **Book** class:

```
package com.gitforgits.model;
import jakarta.persistence.Entity;
import jakarta.persistence.Id;
import jakarta.persistence.GeneratedValue;
import jakarta.persistence.GenerationType;
@Entity
public class Book {
    @Id
    @GeneratedValue(strategy = GenerationType.IDENTITY)
    private Long id;
    private String title;
    private String author;
    private String description;
    // getters and setters
}
```

The **@Entity** annotation identifies this class as a persistent entity. The **@Id** and

@GeneratedValue annotations specify that **id** is the primary key and is generated by the database. Fields like **title**, **author**, and **description** map to columns with default names. Additional annotations like **@Column**, **@Table**, or relationship annotations (**@OneToMany**, **@ManyToOne**, etc.) further refine mapping rules.

Using Spring Data JPA Repositories

Data operations can be performed through repository interfaces that Spring Data JPA provides. With a single interface extending **JpaRepository**, the code gains CRUD (Create, Read, Update, Delete) and pagination capabilities without writing queries. Consider a **BookRepository**:

```
package com.gitforgits.repository;
import org.springframework.data.jpa.repository.JpaRepository;
import com.gitforgits.model.Book;
public interface BookRepository extends JpaRepository<Book,
Long> {
}
```

This repository supports methods like **findAll()**, **findById()**, and **save()** out of the box. Adding custom finder methods such as **List<Book> findByAuthor(String author);** triggers dynamic query generation. If even more control is needed, annotating methods with **@Query** allows JPQL or native SQL queries. By centralizing data operations in these repositories, services and controllers remain focused on business logic, letting the JPA layer handle persistence details.

Integrating Repositories into Services

The service layer handles data access and applies business rules. If you inject the repository into a service class, it clarifies responsibilities and keeps controllers simpler as shown below:

```
package com.gitforgits.service;
import org.springframework.stereotype.Service;
import com.gitforgits.repository.BookRepository;
import com.gitforgits.model.Book;
import java.util.List;
import java.util.Optional;
```

```java
@Service
public class BookService {
    private final BookRepository repository;
    public BookService(BookRepository repository) {
        this.repository = repository;
    }
    public List<Book> getAllBooks() {
        return repository.findAll();
    }
    public Optional<Book> getBook(Long id) {
        return repository.findById(id);
    }
    public Book saveBook(Book book) {
        return repository.save(book);
    }
    public boolean deleteBook(Long id) {
        if (repository.existsById(id)) {
            repository.deleteById(id);
            return true;
        }
        return false;
    }
}
```

Within this service, **`findAll()`**, **`findById()`**, and **`save()`** delegate to the repository. Changes to the underlying database technology or schema do not affect the controller code. If new business rules emerge, they can be implemented here without rewriting repository logic.

Testing Integration

To be sure that your Hibernate and JPA configurations are working, you should run the application and test the endpoints. If a REST controller exposes endpoints for managing books, creating a new book with a POST request to **/api/books** should insert a record into the database. Then check the console log so as to explore the SQL statements generated by Hibernate. Using **spring.jpa.show-sql=true** helps confirm that **INSERT** and **SELECT** queries appear as expected. You can also make use of tools like **curl**, Postman, or a browser to call endpoints and observe responses. If the **Book** entity and repository are defined correctly, the application should store and retrieve data seamlessly.

For more rigorous testing, consider JUnit tests with **@SpringBootTest** and **TestRestTemplate**, or **@DataJpaTest** for repository layer tests. With **@DataJpaTest**, Spring Boot sets up an in-memory database (like H2), loads JPA and Hibernate, and runs tests quickly without external dependencies.

Handling Schema Evolution and Environments

While **ddl-auto=update** is convenient during development, a more controlled approach to schema changes is advisable for production. There are tools like Flyway or Liquibase that manage migrations by applying versioned scripts or changesets. Initially, working with the automatic updates is acceptable, but as the GitforGits application matures, adopting a migration tool prevents surprises and ensures consistent schema updates across environments. In production configurations, setting **ddl-auto=none** and letting migrations handle schema changes avoids unintended alterations. If switching databases is needed, adjusting **application.properties** and the driver dependency suffices. For example, changing the datasource URL and driver from PostgreSQL to MySQL or MariaDB easily re-targets the application to a different database. Hibernate and JPA shield code from vendor-specific SQL, enabling greater flexibility. Also consider caching mechanisms or secondary-level caches for performance if the application handles large datasets. Spring's ecosystem integrates well with these features, providing additional starters and configuration properties.

Advanced JPA Features

If the domain requires complex relationships, JPA annotations can map them. A **@ManyToOne** annotation on a field in **Book** might reference an **Author** entity, establishing a foreign key relationship. Adding **@OneToMany** on **Author** to link multiple **Book** entities back to the **Author** record forms bidirectional relationships. The Hibernate understands these annotations and generates the appropriate SQL for joining tables. And the lazy loading and eager fetching strategies control when related data is loaded, balancing performance and simplicity. The custom queries defined via JPQL or native SQL help when standard **findBy** methods are insufficient. If you use these features, the persistence layer will grow with the domain, and it'll stay easy to understand and maintain.

Transactions and Consistency

Transaction management is another highlight of using JPA and Hibernate with Spring Boot. By default, repository methods interact with the database in transactional contexts. For more control, **@Transactional** annotations on service methods define transactional boundaries. If a service method performs multiple repository calls, either all operations succeed or the entire transaction rollback if an error occurs. This ensures that the database remains consistent, even if a later step fails. Annotating specific methods or classes with **@Transactional** tailors the transaction scope. While simple CRUD operations might rely on defaults, complex operations spanning multiple tables or services benefit from explicit transaction declarations.

Logging and Monitoring

If issues arise, enabling Hibernate's advanced logging provides insights. Adding:

```
logging.level.org.hibernate.SQL=DEBUG
logging.level.org.hibernate.type.descriptor.sql.BasicBinder=TR
ACE
```

to **application.properties** prints queries and parameter values. Monitoring database connections, execution times, and load patterns leads to optimization opportunities. If slow queries are detected, adding indexes or optimizing entity mappings can improve performance. Over time, these insights help fine-tune the persistence layer.

Defining Entities and Relationships

The concept of mapping the Java classes to database tables transforms the domain model into a persistent form. Here, instead of writing queries by hand, annotations on entity classes control how Hibernate and JPA store and retrieve objects. Entities represent the core data elements, while relationships define how these entities connect. A scenario like GitforGits often involves multiple related tables—perhaps books and authors, or publishers and categories. By annotating fields with **@OneToMany**, **@ManyToOne**, **@ManyToMany**, and similar annotations, the code describes how objects relate. And, the Hibernate uses this information to generate join tables, foreign keys, and queries that load associated data.

Let us start with a simple **Author** entity, consider something like the below one:

```
package com.gitforgits.model;
import jakarta.persistence.Entity;
import jakarta.persistence.Id;
import jakarta.persistence.GeneratedValue;
```

```
import jakarta.persistence.GenerationType;
import jakarta.persistence.OneToMany;
import java.util.List;
@Entity
public class Author {
    @Id
    @GeneratedValue(strategy = GenerationType.IDENTITY)
    private Long id;
    private String name;
    private String biography;
    @OneToMany(mappedBy = "author")
    private List<Book> books;
    // getters and setters
}
```

Here, defining **Author** and giving it a **List<Book>** field annotated with **@OneToMany(mappedBy = "author")**, the code expresses a one-to-many relationship: one author writes many books. The **mappedBy** attribute points to the field in the **Book** entity that owns the relationship. It instructs Hibernate that **Author** is not the table containing the foreign key; the **Book** entity's **author** field holds the foreign key column. This prevents confusion and clarifies ownership of the relationship.

On the **Book** side:

```
package com.gitforgits.model;
import jakarta.persistence.Entity;
import jakarta.persistence.Id;
import jakarta.persistence.GeneratedValue;
import jakarta.persistence.GenerationType;
import jakarta.persistence.ManyToOne;
@Entity
public class Book {
    @Id
```

```
    @GeneratedValue(strategy = GenerationType.IDENTITY)
    private Long id;
    private String title;
    private String description;
    @ManyToOne
    private Author author;
    // getters and setters
}
```

After annotating the **author** field in **Book** with **@ManyToOne**, the code states that many books can link to one author. Hibernate creates a column like **author_id** in the **book** table to store the primary key of the related author. When we load a book, Hibernate can fetch the associated author. When we save a book with an assigned author, it updates the foreign key column. The **mappedBy** attribute in **Author** ensures that the **author** field in **Book** is considered the owning side. By default, a **ManyToOne** relationship belongs to the entity that has the foreign key field.

\nother common scenario involves many-to-many relationships. For instance, if a book can have ıultiple categories, and a category can contain multiple books, the relationship forms a many-to-ıny pattern. In relational databases, this usually requires a join table. Without writing SQL to ate such a table, using **@ManyToMany** instructs Hibernate to handle it. Consider a **tegory** entity:

```
kage com.gitforgits.model;
 rt jakarta.persistence.Entity;
 :t jakarta.persistence.Id;
  t jakarta.persistence.GeneratedValue;
    jakarta.persistence.GenerationType;
    jakarta.persistence.ManyToMany;
    java.util.List;

     lass Category {

      -atedValue(strategy = GenerationType.IDENTITY)
```

```
    private Long id;
    private String name;
    @ManyToMany(mappedBy = "categories")
    private List<Book> books;
    // getters and setters
}
```

Now, modify **Book** to include **categories**:

```
@ManyToMany
private List<Category> categories;
```

To define a many-to-many relationship properly, at least one side should specify the **mappedBy** attribute. This avoids generating multiple join tables. If we decide **Book** owns the relationship, we might write:

```
@ManyToMany
@JoinTable(
    name = "book_category",
    joinColumns = @JoinColumn(name = "book_id"),
    inverseJoinColumns = @JoinColumn(name = "category_id")
)
private List<Category> categories;
```

Then in **Category**:

```
@ManyToMany(mappedBy = "categories")
private List<Book> books;
```

This configuration creates a **book_category** join table with **book_id** and **category_id** columns. Adding or removing categories from a book modifies entries in the join table. Loading a book fetches associated categories if needed. The **mappedBy** side (**Category** in this case) references the field in **Book** that owns the relationship.

For more complex relationships, **@OneToOne** and **@ManyToMany** mappings handle special cases. A one-to-one relationship might appear if each book has a unique detail record:

```java
@Entity
public class BookDetail {
    @Id
    @GeneratedValue(strategy = GenerationType.IDENTITY)
    private Long id;
    private String isbn;
    private int pages;
    @OneToOne(mappedBy = "detail")
    private Book book;
}
// In Book:
@OneToOne
@JoinColumn(name = "detail_id")
private BookDetail detail;
```

This sets a foreign key **`detail_id`** in the **`book`** table, linking each book to a unique detail record.

When working with relationships, consider fetch strategies. By default, many-to-one relationships are eagerly fetched, meaning when a book is loaded, the author is also loaded. One-to-many and many-to-many defaults often differ. Using **`fetch = FetchType.LAZY`** or **`fetch = FetchType.EAGER`** influences when related data is retrieved. Lazy loading defers the fetching of related entities until needed, improving performance and reducing initial query complexity. If a field is rarely accessed, lazy fetching prevents unnecessary overhead. Eager fetching ensures immediate availability of related data but can cause large queries and slowdowns if many entities load at once.

Testing these mappings involves running the application and using repository methods or controllers to create, retrieve, and update entities. For instance, inserting a new author and then creating several books linked to that author demonstrates whether foreign keys and relationships are persisted correctly. Queries like **`repository.findAll()`** retrieve authors with their books if eagerly loaded, or trigger lazy loading when accessing **`getBooks()`** for the first time. Logging SQL to the console helps confirm that join queries execute as expected. As relationships grow in complexity, adding indexes and tuning queries becomes important. JPA annotations and **`@Entity`** mappings remain flexible. Renaming fields or changing relationships typically only requires updating annotations and perhaps adjusting join columns. Unlike raw SQL, code changes remain localized to the entity classes, preserving readability.

Implementing Repositories

After defining entities and relationships, implementing repositories ensures easy data access. By leveraging Spring Data JPA, we avoid writing boilerplate data access code. Instead, repository interfaces provide CRUD operations, query derivation from method names, and customization options with **@Query** annotations. The service and controller layers use these repositories for domain logic and HTTP endpoints, leaving persistence details hidden behind a simple API.

To create a repository for the **Author** entity:

```
package com.gitforgits.repository;

import org.springframework.data.jpa.repository.JpaRepository;

import com.gitforgits.model.Author;

public interface AuthorRepository extends
JpaRepository<Author, Long> {

}
```

This interface extends **JpaRepository<Author, Long>** where **Author** is the entity type and **Long** the primary key type. Without additional methods, we gain **findAll()**, **findById(Long id)**, **save(Author author)**, and **deleteById(Long id)** automatically. Calling **authorRepository.findAll()** returns a List of all authors, **authorRepository.findById(1L)** returns an Optional containing the author with ID 1 if it exists, and **authorRepository.save(author)** inserts or updates a record. Similar repositories for **Book** and **Category** can be created:

```
public interface BookRepository extends JpaRepository<Book,
Long> {

    List<Book> findByTitle(String title);

}
```

If we need to find books by title, adding **findByTitle(String title)** lets Spring Data derive a query: **SELECT b FROM Book b WHERE b.title = :title**. For partial matches, **List<Book> findByTitleContaining(String keyword);** generates a query like **SELECT b FROM Book b WHERE b.title LIKE %:keyword%**. More complex filtering can be achieved with multiple conditions, such as **List<Book> findByAuthorName(String name);** which, if properly mapped, becomes **SELECT b FROM Book b WHERE b.author.name = :name**.

If the derived queries are insufficient, **@Query** annotations allow specifying JPQL or native SQL:

```
@Query("SELECT b FROM Book b JOIN b.categories c WHERE c.name = :categoryName")
List<Book> findBooksByCategoryName(String categoryName);
```

This method retrieves books belonging to a given category. Spring Data JPA parses the **@Query** annotation and sets parameters automatically. If exact entity names or field names change, updating the JPQL string suffices. The rest of the code remains stable. The repositories integrate seamlessly with the service layer. For example, a **CategoryService** class might look like:

```
package com.gitforgits.service;
import org.springframework.stereotype.Service;
import com.gitforgits.repository.CategoryRepository;
import com.gitforgits.model.Category;
import java.util.List;
@Service
public class CategoryService {
    private final CategoryRepository repository;
    public CategoryService(CategoryRepository repository) {
        this.repository = repository;
    }
    public List<Category> getAllCategories() {
        return repository.findAll();
    }
    public Category createCategory(Category category) {
        return repository.save(category);
    }
    public List<Category> getBooksByCategoryName(String categoryName) {
        // If we need to call a repository method that returns books, place it in BookRepository
        // or consider a custom query here if cross-repository logic is needed.
```

```
        return repository.findAll(); // placeholder until a
real method is implemented
    }
}
```

If cross-referencing between repositories is required, either inject multiple repositories into a single service or create a specialized repository method that returns the needed data. For example, if **BookRepository** has **findBooksByCategoryName(String categoryName)**, the service can call that method directly to get books in a category. The goal is to keep controllers lean by deferring logic to services, and keep services simple by relying on repository queries instead of handcrafting SQL.

Another advantage of repositories is that they simplify testing. If **@DataJpaTest** is used, Spring Boot sets up an in-memory database and scans for entities and repositories. Running tests against repository methods validates that the mappings and queries work as intended. If a test inserts a few **Author** and **Book** entities, calling **bookRepository.findByAuthorName("John Doe")** checks whether the query logic and relationship mappings are correct. A passing test indicates that no manual SQL or low-level JDBC handling is necessary. The repository interfaces can also integrate with pagination and sorting by extending **PagingAndSortingRepository** or using **Pageable** and **Sort** arguments in query methods. For example, **Page<Book> findByAuthorName(String name, Pageable pageable);** retrieves a slice of books matching the author's name. This feature supports building scalable APIs that return paginated results, improving performance and user experience.

When applying changes to relationships, simply adjusting entities and repository queries can help. If a new relationship is introduced, adding or modifying repository methods might be enough to retrieve related data. If the naming conventions do not yield a suitable derived query, define a custom **@Query** to reflect the new structure. In some cases, custom repository implementations can add behavior not covered by derived queries or **@Query** annotations. Creating a custom repository interface and implementation class allows writing custom code, perhaps using the **EntityManager** directly. This might be necessary for batch updates, complex joins, or vendor-specific SQL optimizations. Still, these scenarios are less common, and the default Spring Data JPA features handle most typical data access patterns.

Summary

With this, you have learned how to define entities and model relationships in a Spring Boot application using JPA and Hibernate. You saw how Java classes were annotated with @Entity and how primary keys and generated values represented database identities. You get to observe how one-to-many and many-to-many relationships allowed expressing associations between domain objects without writing explicit SQL join statements. This approach had made it simpler to evolve the domain model and maintain data integrity as the application grew.

Next, you explored implementing repositories using Spring Data JPA. You had discovered that extending JpaRepository interfaces gave you built-in CRUD operations, query derivation from method names, and the option to write custom queries with @Query. By integrating repositories into the service layer, you had kept controllers lean and had separated business logic from persistence details. You had tested these layers by running the application, using HTTP endpoints to create and retrieve data, and verifying that relationships and queries functioned correctly. Through these steps, you have developed a maintainable and flexible persistence layer aligned with your evolving domain model.

CHAPTER 6: MANAGING DATABASE INTERACTIONS

Database Configuration and Connectivity

Having a reliable data source is a key part of building a solid backend application. If you can make sure the code can connect to the database and keep that connection, you'll be able to get data, make updates, and store it all smoothly. With Spring Boot, a lot of this configuration effort is made easier by auto-configuration features. You just set a few properties, and the environment automatically detects and initializes the required beans for connecting to the database. This leaves the domain logic unaffected by low-level connection details.

Setting Data Source Properties

First, make sure the PostgreSQL server is up and running and you can access it. Usually, a local PostgreSQL instance is set up on the default port for development. It's also a good idea to create a dedicated database for the GitforGits project, so you have a clean environment. For example, use **`createdb gitforgitsdb`** from the command line if supported, and verify that a user, say **`gitforgitsuser`**, has the necessary permissions. Once the database and user are ready, open **`src/main/resources/application.properties`** or **`application.yml`** to specify connection details:

```
spring.datasource.url=jdbc:postgresql://localhost:5432/gitforg
itsdb
spring.datasource.username=gitforgitsuser
spring.datasource.password=yourpassword
spring.jpa.hibernate.ddl-auto=update
spring.jpa.show-sql=true
```

These properties inform Spring Boot which URL, username, and password to use. With **`spring.jpa.hibernate.ddl-auto=update`**, the schema updates automatically to match entity definitions during development. The **`show-sql=true`** property prints SQL statements to the console, aiding debugging and understanding of the underlying queries.

Verifying Connections

After applying the properties, run the application. If everything is correct, Spring Boot establishes a **`DataSource`** and an **`EntityManagerFactory`** at startup. The logs should show no errors related to connectivity. If a **`PSQLException`** appears, double-check credentials, database existence, or firewall rules. In cases where PostgreSQL runs on a remote machine or a different port, adjust the URL accordingly. For example:

```
spring.datasource.url=jdbc:postgresql://remotehost:5433/gitfor
gitsdb
```

If authentication fails, ensure the username and password match the PostgreSQL roles configured via **psql** or a database admin tool. Verifying credentials at the psql prompt (**psql -h localhost -U gitforgitsuser gitforgitsdb**) can confirm that access rights are correct.

Profile-specific Configurations

The separation of environment-specific configurations often proves beneficial. For instance, **application-dev.properties** could hold development settings while **application-prod.properties** might define production connections. If we set the **spring.profiles.active=dev** at runtime, it then activates the development profile. The different URLs, credentials, or logging levels can then be managed without manual file edits before each deployment. This approach simplifies moving from local development to production hosting, where the database might reside on a different server.

Using YAML for Configuration

While **.properties** files work fine, switching to **application.yml** might improve readability:

```
spring:
  datasource:
    url: jdbc:postgresql://localhost:5432/gitforgitsdb
    username: gitforgitsuser
    password: yourpassword
  jpa:
    hibernate:
      ddl-auto: update
    show-sql: true
```

This format nests related properties, making it clear how various pieces connect. Both **.properties** and **.yml** files achieve the same result, so choose whichever format feels more natural.

Adapting to Different Environments

If we deploy to the cloud or another external environment, then only the URL and credentials may need to change. A managed PostgreSQL service might provide a URL like **jdbc:postgresql://mydb.gitforgits.com:5432/gitforgitsdb** and credentials stored in environment variables. Using the below placeholders:

```
spring.datasource.url=${DB_URL}
spring.datasource.username=${DB_USER}
spring.datasource.password=${DB_PASS}
```

enables injecting credentials at runtime without hardcoding them. This approach prevents sensitive data from being committed to version control, improving security.

Connection Pooling and Advanced Settings

Spring Boot often uses HikariCP as a default connection pool. Connection pools maintain a set of ready-to-use connections, reducing overhead when handling multiple requests. If fine-tuning is needed, properties like:

```
spring.datasource.hikari.maximum-pool-size=10
```

control pool size. Increasing or decreasing the pool size affects performance and resource usage. Monitoring load and adjusting these values ensures smooth operation. If SSL connections or custom parameters are needed, appending **?ssl=true** or other options to the URL might suffice. Checking PostgreSQL driver documentation clarifies advanced configurations. Each scenario differs, but Spring Boot's flexibility accommodates multiple options.

Testing Connectivity and Queries

To confirm the configuration, consider writing an integration test. Using **@SpringBootTest** on a test class that autowire a repository and calls **findAll()** can confirm queries run successfully. If the test passes, connectivity and configuration likely work correctly. If not, logs and exceptions direct the troubleshooting. The adjustment of properties, verifying database status, or checking firewall rules resolves most issues quickly.

For local development convenience, an in-memory database like H2 might also be used in tests, specified via **test** profile configurations. Switching between PostgreSQL and H2 for tests depends on environment properties. By focusing on a single data source configuration first, the fundamentals become clearer before introducing complexity.

Considering Migrations and Environments

Though **ddl-auto=update** saves time during development, production environments often rely on migration tools like Flyway or Liquibase. These tools apply scripted changesets to keep the schema synchronized with entity definitions safely. However, stable database connectivity underpins even these migrations. Since we know the connection works, developers can focus on controlled schema evolution without fretting about startup issues blocking migrations.

As complexity increases, consider running multiple data sources if the application interacts with different databases. In such advanced cases, defining beans for each **DataSource** and **EntityManagerFactory** can isolate modules. For now, a single PostgreSQL instance suffices.

Adapting to Other Databases

If switching from PostgreSQL to another relational database like MySQL, changing the URL, driver dependency, and possibly credentials adapts the application. JPA and Hibernate remain database-agnostic, so minimal code changes are needed. Only vendor-specific features or query hints might require minor adjustments.

Ensuring stable connectivity and proper configuration lays a foundation for managing database interactions. With a **DataSource** established, repositories and entities can perform CRUD operations smoothly. Proper pooling and environment-specific profiles let the application adapt to various deployment scenarios, from local development to production clusters. This flexibility ensures that as the domain model and user base grow, the application retains reliable, scalable access to persistent data.

CRUD Operations with Repositories

Previously, we introduced the concepts of Create, Read, Update, and Delete to handle data within the application's domain. At that time, we focused on how HTTP methods like GET, POST, PUT, and DELETE mapped onto these operations and how REST endpoints interacted with the service and repository layers. At this stage, a reminder that we already covered how controllers and services orchestrated these actions suffices. Rather than re-teaching the underlying theory, it now helps to see how repository methods translate these actions directly into database operations.

Here, let us consider the **BookRepository** interface, which likely extends **JpaRepository<Book, Long>**. With no extra configuration, it already provides methods for CRUD:

- **save(entity)**: Insert or update a record. If the entity has no ID, it inserts. If it does, it updates the existing row.
- **findById(id)**: Retrieve a single record by primary key, returning an Optional.
- **findAll()**: Load all records of that entity type.

- **deleteById(id)**: Remove a record by its primary key.
- **delete(entity)**: Remove a specific entity instance.

To perform create operations, call **save()** with a new entity object. For example, if the **Book** entity represents a record in the database, a snippet in the service layer might look like this:

```
public Book createBook(Book book) {
    return bookRepository.save(book);
}
```

This single call inserts a new row into the database if the **book** object lacks an ID. Spring Data JPA inspects the entity and uses Hibernate to run an INSERT statement. If the database auto-generates the primary key, that ID appears in the returned entity. The service can then return it to the controller, which sends it back to the client as a JSON response.

For read operations, **findById(id)** returns an Optional. The service can handle the absence of a record gracefully:

```
public Optional<Book> getBook(Long id) {
    return bookRepository.findById(id);
}
```

If a record with that ID exists, the Optional contains it. If not, the Optional is empty. The controller can return a 404 response if the Optional is empty, or a 200 with the found entity if it's present. For listing multiple entries, **findAll()** retrieves every record of that entity, returning a List. This allows the service layer to provide full sets of data or filtered subsets if custom queries are introduced later.

The update of records involves calling **save()** again, but this time on an entity that already has an ID. For example:

```
public Optional<Book> updateBook(Long id, Book updatedData) {
    return bookRepository.findById(id).map(existing -> {
        existing.setTitle(updatedData.getTitle());
        existing.setAuthor(updatedData.getAuthor());
        existing.setDescription(updatedData.getDescription());
        return bookRepository.save(existing);
    });
```

```
}
```

In the above sample code, the code first fetches the existing record. If present, it adjusts fields and calls **`save()`** again. Since **`existing`** already has an ID, Hibernate issues an UPDATE statement. If not found, the Optional remains empty, and no update occurs. Finally, deleting records with **`deleteById(id)`** or **`delete(entity)`** removes them from the database:

```
public boolean deleteBook(Long id) {
    if (bookRepository.existsById(id)) {
        bookRepository.deleteById(id);
        return true;
    }
    return false;
}
```

Calling **`deleteById()`** issues a DELETE statement. If the record doesn't exist, no changes occur. The boolean return value indicates success or failure, letting controllers respond accordingly. All these repository methods encapsulate CRUD operations cleanly. Without writing SQL or dealing with the JDBC API directly, data modifications remain straightforward. Custom queries, either derived from method names (like **`findByTitle(String title)`**) or defined with **`@Query`**, extend beyond basic CRUD without changing this fundamental approach.

Transaction Management

As we add more and more steps to a project, we might need to do a bunch of queries in a row. For example, one service method might create a book and insert related author data at the same time. If one insert succeeds and the other fails, the database could end up in an inconsistent state. Transaction management makes sure that these sets of operations either all succeed or all fail together, keeping your data consistent. Usually, simple CRUD operations run in their own transactions or use default settings. But Spring and JPA give you explicit control over transactions.

Introduction to @Transactional

Placing the **`@Transactional`** annotation at the class or method level informs Spring that the enclosed operations should run within a single transaction boundary. If all operations complete successfully, the transaction commits, applying all changes to the database. If an exception is thrown, the transaction rollback, discarding any partial changes. This approach eliminates partial updates and inconsistent data states. For services that perform complex operations involving multiple repositories or queries, **@Transactional** ensures atomicity.

A typical usage might be:

```
import
org.springframework.transaction.annotation.Transactional;
@Service
public class PublishingService {
    private final BookRepository bookRepository;
    private final AuthorRepository authorRepository;
    public PublishingService(BookRepository bookRepository,
AuthorRepository authorRepository) {
        this.bookRepository = bookRepository;
        this.authorRepository = authorRepository;
    }
    @Transactional
    public Book publishBookWithAuthor(Book book, Author
author) {
        Author savedAuthor = authorRepository.save(author);
        book.setAuthor(savedAuthor);
        return bookRepository.save(book);
    }
}
```

Here, in the above code, both the **authorRepository.save(author)** and **bookRepository.save(book)** calls execute within one transaction. If the second save fails due to a constraint violation, the entire transaction rollback, and the database remains unchanged. If both succeed, the transaction commits, guaranteeing that both book and author records appear together in a consistent state.

Default Transactional Behavior

When using **spring-boot-starter-data-jpa**, some operations might run within a transactional context by default. For example, repository save methods often execute in a transaction. However, relying solely on defaults can be risky if operations span multiple repositories or multiple calls that need atomicity. By explicitly adding **@Transactional** to service methods, the code expresses intent more clearly and simplifies reasoning about when a commit or rollback happens.

The **@Transactional** can be placed on a class so that all methods are transactional, or on individual methods for finer control. Class-level annotations apply to all public methods unless overridden by a method-level annotation. If some operations do not need a transaction, they can remain unannotated or use a read-only hint.

Controlling Transaction Scope and Isolation

By default, the **@Transactional** marks methods as transactional with default isolation and propagation settings. Isolation levels determine how concurrent transactions interact. For example, **@Transactional(isolation = Isolation.SERIALIZABLE)** imposes stricter rules on concurrent reads and writes, avoiding anomalies but reducing parallelism. Propagation levels, like **Propagation.REQUIRES_NEW**, define how nested calls behave. If a method annotated with **REQUIRES_NEW** is called within an existing transaction, it suspends the current one and starts a fresh transaction.

For most simple applications, the default isolation and propagation suffice. If complexity grows, adjusting these parameters ensures transactions behave as needed. For instance, a complex publishing workflow that involves multiple steps might require **REQUIRES_NEW** for certain steps to ensure partial failures do not roll back the entire process.

Rollback Rules

By default, runtime exceptions trigger rollbacks. Checked exceptions might not cause a rollback unless configured explicitly. If a service method throws a **RuntimeException**, the transaction rollback. If it throws a checked exception and you want a rollback to occur, specify this in **@Transactional**:

```
@Transactional(rollbackFor = { IOException.class })
public void performFileLinkedDatabaseUpdate() throws
IOException {
    // If something here throws IOException, rollback occurs.
}
```

This above configuration ensures that even checked exceptions prompt a rollback, preserving consistency. If desired, you can also specify exceptions that should not cause rollbacks with **noRollbackFor**.

Testing Transactions

Generally, the integration tests are able to verify transactional behavior. A test that triggers an exception after partially updating the database should leave no partial changes if **@Transactional** is working correctly. One can insert a record, cause an error intentionally, and then query the database to confirm that no record remains. This approach ensures that transaction boundaries match expectations.

If tests run with **@Transactional** at the test class level, changes often roll back after each test. This strategy keeps the test database clean and ensures tests start with a known state. However, if verifying that commits persist data is necessary, consider disabling transactional tests or using a separate test method annotated differently. Another approach involves checking database state within the same transaction as the test to confirm behavior.

Performance and Transaction Handling

Transactions come with overhead. Keeping them brief and focused on necessary operations helps performance. Long-running transactions can lock rows, slow concurrency, or cause contention. Breaking large operations into multiple steps or using appropriate isolation levels avoids performance bottlenecks. If certain read-only queries do not need a transaction, marking them as **@Transactional(readOnly = true)** can permit the database to optimize execution. Although Hibernate might still open a session, read-only hints prevent unneeded dirty checks or updates.

When dealing with caching or second-level caches, transactions ensure consistency between cached objects and the database. If multiple updates occur inside a transaction, the commit flushes changes to the database, and Hibernate updates caches accordingly. Without transactions, caches or other frameworks might not synchronize correctly.

Combining Transactions with Other Features

As features like batch operations, messaging integrations, or distributed transactions emerge, controlling transaction boundaries remains central. For example, if one must send a message to a queue only after a database commit, placing messaging logic after the transaction commits ensures that no message is sent when the database fails to persist changes. Alternatively, using **TransactionSynchronizationManager** or related hooks can run code after a commit completes.

If using multiple data sources, **@Transactional** can specify which transaction manager to use. This flexibility allows distinct transaction boundaries per data source if needed. Although this scenario is advanced, knowing that **@Transactional** supports multiple transaction managers helps scale more complex architectures. The transaction management with **@Transactional** gives clear control over atomic operations. It ensures that sets of changes either fully apply or not at all, protecting against partial updates and data inconsistencies. By integrating this tool with CRUD operations and repository interactions, we maintain a stable environment as complexity grows.

Querying with JPQL and Criteria API

Complex applications often demand flexible querying capabilities that exceed basic CRUD and simple finder methods. While derived queries and **@Query** annotations solve many problems, certain scenarios call for more expressive and dynamic query-building techniques. For instance, imagine a scenario where the GitforGits project must find books filtered by multiple conditions that may vary at runtime. A user might request all books by a certain author, published after a certain year, containing a particular keyword in the title, and belonging to multiple categories. Hardcoding all these conditions into a single repository method name or a fixed **@Query** annotation may not be practical. Similarly, building dynamic SQL strings by concatenation can lead to brittle, error-prone code. The Java Persistence Query Language (JPQL) and the Criteria API provide structured and type-safe ways to construct, parameterize, and execute complex queries.

Using JPQL for Complex Queries

JPQL is a string-based query language similar to SQL, but it works at the entity level rather than directly referencing tables. It uses entity class and field names instead of table and column names. Writing a JPQL query feels like writing SQL, but references to entities and their relationships make queries more object-oriented.

Let us take an example of retrieving all books by a certain author's name which might look like:

```
@Query("SELECT b FROM Book b WHERE b.author.name =
:authorName")
List<Book> findBooksByAuthorName(@Param("authorName") String
authorName);
```

This **@Query** annotation expresses a JPQL query. It selects from the entity **Book**, not the **book** table, and uses the **author.name** field instead of a column name. JPQL handles joins based on relationships automatically. If conditions grow more complicated, such as filtering by year and category, extending JPQL might involve adding more predicates:

```
@Query("SELECT b FROM Book b JOIN b.categories c WHERE
b.author.name = :authorName AND b.publicationYear > :year AND
c.name IN :categories")
```

```
List<Book>
findBooksByAuthorAndYearAndCategories(@Param("authorName")
String authorName, @Param("year") int year,
@Param("categories") List<String> categories);
```

This approach works, but hardcoding complex queries may become unwieldy if conditions vary at runtime. If each parameter is optional, building multiple **@Query** methods for every combination is not ideal. A more dynamic solution is needed, which is where the Criteria API comes in.

Criteria API for Dynamic Queries

The Criteria API lets you build queries at runtime in a programmatic, type-safe way. Instead of writing JPQL strings, you can use a fluent API to define selects, joins, and predicates. This lets you add conditions based on things like what the user inputs or other factors. For example, sometimes we filter by author name, sometimes by year, and sometimes by categories, depending on which parameters the user supplies. The Criteria API lets you build the query step-by-step.

The setup of a criteria query involves accessing the **EntityManager**. Although repositories abstract many details away, custom repository implementations can inject an **EntityManager** to run Criteria queries.

Let us take an example:

```
import jakarta.persistence.EntityManager;
import jakarta.persistence.PersistenceContext;
import jakarta.persistence.criteria.*;
@Repository
public class BookCustomRepository {
    @PersistenceContext
    private EntityManager em;
    public List<Book> findBooksDynamically(String authorName,
Integer year, List<String> categories) {
        CriteriaBuilder cb = em.getCriteriaBuilder();
        CriteriaQuery<Book> cq = cb.createQuery(Book.class);
        Root<Book> bookRoot = cq.from(Book.class);
        // Start building predicates
```

```
        List<Predicate> predicates = new ArrayList<>();
        if (authorName != null) {

predicates.add(cb.equal(bookRoot.get("author").get("name"),
authorName));
        }
        if (year != null) {

predicates.add(cb.greaterThan(bookRoot.get("publicationYear"),
year));
        }
        if (categories != null && !categories.isEmpty()) {
            Join<Book, Category> categoryJoin =
bookRoot.join("categories");

predicates.add(categoryJoin.get("name").in(categories));
        }
        cq.select(bookRoot).where(predicates.toArray(new
Predicate[0]));
        return em.createQuery(cq).getResultList();
    }
}
```

This code creates a **CriteriaBuilder** from the **EntityManager** and starts building a **CriteriaQuery**. It selects from the **Book** entity. Predicates are collected in a list, and only added if the corresponding parameter is provided. For example, if **authorName** is null, no predicate is added for the author's name. If **categories** is empty, no category predicate is included. The **where** clause uses all collected predicates, forming a flexible query that adapts to runtime conditions. Executing **em.createQuery(cq).getResultList()** returns the results.

Here, the code becomes more verbose than a simple **@Query** annotation, but this trade-off provides flexibility. If a field is renamed in the entity class, a Java compiler error might occur at the Criteria building step, rather than silently failing at runtime. Some queries might require partial projections or aggregate functions. JPQL supports aggregate functions like **COUNT**, **AVG**, **MAX**, and **MIN**. Criteria also supports constructing expressions for these aggregates. For example, counting how many books an author has published might involve selecting **cb.count(bookRoot)**. If returning a custom DTO instead of an entity is necessary, JPQL and Criteria queries can select tuples or specify constructors in JPQL queries. The Criteria API can build a **CriteriaQuery<Tuple>** or **CriteriaQuery<Object[]>** and map results manually.

Summary

To sum it up, you learned how to configure data sources and connect your application to a PostgreSQL database. You set properties in application configuration files, and Spring Boot automatically created the required DataSource and integrated it with Hibernate and JPA. You saw that tweaking settings like username, password, and URL lets the app connect to different environments. You also figured out that you could automate schema building through properties, but that controlled migrations were necessary for production scenarios.

Next, you then refreshed the concepts of CRUD operations and understood how repository methods could persist and retrieve data. You also saw that using **@Transactional** with **@Query** keeps things atomic and consistent when multiple operations need to happen together. You also saw that runtime exceptions triggered automatic rollbacks and that parameters in **@Transactional** could alter this behavior. Lastly, you figured out how to make complex queries using JPQL and the Criteria API, which lets you retrieve data in flexible and dynamic ways, even when the filtering requirements are complicated.

CHAPTER 7: USER AUTHENTICATION AND AUTHORIZATION WITH SPRING SECURITY

Introduction to Spring Security

When building a strong backend, you've got to be handling sensitive data and making sure that only the people who need it can access it. If you let everyone access every endpoint without checking who they are first, it could leave the system open to abuse and unauthorized access. To keep things safe, it's crucial to use a security setup that works smoothly with Spring Boot and gives you the freedom to adjust settings according to your needs.

The whole point of authentication is to make sure that only the right users can access protected resources. It's better to keep protected data from people who haven't logged in with Spring Security. This means collecting credentials (often a username and password) and verifying them against a user store or identity provider. Then, authorization determines what authenticated users can do once they're inside the system. While authentication confirms who a user is, authorization makes sure they have the right permissions to perform certain actions. Together, these concepts make sure that sensitive endpoints and operations are only available to those who meet the defined security policies.

So, Spring Security works by building on the standard HTTP interaction model, which means it intercepts requests even before they reach the controller layer. It configures a security filter chain to decide whether a request needs to be authenticated and, if so, prompts the user to supply credentials. Once the user is confirmed, the requests carry a security context that includes info about the user and their permissions. Then, the controllers and services can use that info to decide if the user is allowed to do the operations they've requested. Since Spring Security works so well with the whole Spring stack, it's a piece of cake to set up custom authentication sources (like databases, LDAP directories, or third-party identity providers), encryption algorithms, password encoders, and session policies.

At its core, Spring Security acts as a chain of filters placed in front of the application's endpoints. Each filter in the chain either confirms authentication, initiates login flows, or applies authorization checks. For example, the **`UsernamePasswordAuthenticationFilter`** extracts login credentials from a request, passes them to an authentication manager for verification, and, upon success, stores user details in the security context. Subsequent filters or components can then rely on this established identity to allow or deny actions. While this may sound complex, Spring Boot's auto-configuration and starter dependencies often provide sensible defaults, requiring minimal setup to secure endpoints.

One common pattern involves using a database to store user credentials and roles. Spring Security's **`UserDetailsService`** interface and related classes simplify loading user details from a data source, while password encoders manage hashing and comparing stored passwords. Instead of storing plain-text passwords, a secure hashing algorithm ensures that even if the database is compromised, attackers cannot easily recover user passwords. By default, Spring Security supports modern password encoders that implement secure hashing functions, making it simple to protect user credentials effectively.

Another advantage lies in how flexible and configurable Spring Security is. If basic username and password authentication is insufficient, integrating with OAuth 2.0 or OpenID Connect providers is possible. This approach delegates authentication to external identity providers (like Google or GitHub), enabling single sign-on and more sophisticated security flows. Similarly, applying method-level security allows restricting certain methods within service classes to users with specific roles or authorities using annotations like **`@PreAuthorize`** or **`@RolesAllowed`**. By stacking these features together, the security configuration can grow and adapt as the application's requirements evolve.

Spring Security's authorization model often revolves around roles and authorities. A role might be a high-level category like "ADMIN" or "USER," while authorities could represent more granular permissions. Checking a user's role ensures that only users in a certain group can access a given endpoint, while authority checks might allow fine-grained control. For instance, all "ADMIN" users might access administrative endpoints, while only those with a specific "BOOK_WRITE" authority can create or modify book records. This tiered approach lets you tailor security to the application's domain model and operational needs, granting precisely the level of access each user requires—no more, no less.

Implementing Spring Security in a Spring Boot application generally involves adding the **`spring-boot-starter-security`** dependency and then customizing the default configuration. By default, Spring Security locks down all endpoints, requiring a username and password. Adjusting these defaults might mean allowing some endpoints to remain public (like a homepage or a login page) while protecting others. A typical security configuration class (annotated with **`@EnableWebSecurity`**) defines which endpoints are secured, what authentication mechanism is used, and how login and logout are handled.

A common scenario might look like this: when a user tries to access a protected endpoint, Spring Security checks if they are already authenticated. If not, it may redirect them to a login page or return a 401 response prompting them to authenticate. After successful login, the user's session holds their identity, and future requests within that session skip the login requirement. If the user tries to access an endpoint they are not authorized for, Spring Security returns a 403 response. Through these standard HTTP status codes and flows, clients understand when authentication or authorization is missing or insufficient.

In a REST API scenario, where statelessness often takes priority, Spring Security can handle stateless authentication approaches as well. Instead of sessions, an API might rely on tokens or JWTs (JSON Web Tokens) that the client includes in each request. Spring Security can integrate with token-based approaches, parsing and validating tokens to authenticate requests without storing session state. This pattern suits microservices architectures or any scenario where the client (such as a single-page application or mobile app) handles its own session logic.

As we move forward with implementing Spring Security in our GitforGits project, the first steps involve adding the necessary dependencies and creating a security configuration class. In the following sections, we will define how users log in, how their credentials are stored and validated, and which endpoints require authentication. Once authenticated users are established, we can assign roles or authorities, restricting certain actions (like adding new books or editing author details) to authorized users only. This layered approach ensures that the application not only identifies who the user is but also enforces what they can or cannot do. Once authentication is working, we can apply authorization checks to specific endpoints. For instance, only users with an "ADMIN" role might access administrative endpoints that manage books and authors, while general "USER" roles might only read public data. Spring Security's DSL (Domain Specific Language) for HTTP security configuration—available through classes like **`HttpSecurity`**—provides a fluent syntax for specifying these rules. For example, **`http.authorizeRequests().antMatchers("/admin/**").hasRole("ADMIN")`** ensures that any request to the **`/admin`** path requires the "ADMIN" role.

Implementing Authentication Mechanisms

After understanding how Spring Security fits into the application, the next step is to implement the authentication mechanisms practically. We now begin with adding the **`spring-boot-starter-security`** dependency to the project's **`pom.xml`**. Once included, restarting the application often causes all endpoints to become protected by default. At this stage, a default user and password appear in the logs. While this default behavior proves that security is active, a custom configuration is needed for real scenarios. By defining a security configuration class, we take control over authentication and authorization rules.

Defining Security Configuration Class

Creating a **`SecurityConfig`** class annotated with **`@Configuration`** and returning a **`SecurityFilterChain`** bean allows specifying how requests should be secured. Calling methods like **`authorizeHttpRequests()`**, **`antMatchers()`**, and **`formLogin()`** tailors the security rules. For instance, permitting **`/public/**`** paths without authentication and protecting all others ensures only authenticated users can reach sensitive endpoints. Using **`httpBasic()`** and **`formLogin()`** sets up basic authentication and a login form respectively. Although basic or form-based logins are initial steps, the configuration can evolve toward token-based authentication as needs change.

Creating In-memory User Store

To quickly test authentication, consider using an in-memory user store. Defining a **`UserDetailsService`** bean that returns an **`InMemoryUserDetailsManager`** populated with a few users and roles proves that the configuration works. For instance, a user named "john" with role "USER" and another named "admin" with role "ADMIN" lets you log in to restricted endpoints. Encoding passwords with a **`PasswordEncoder`** ensures passwords are never stored in plain text. Although in-memory users are not suitable for production, this approach confirms that authentication logic functions correctly before integrating a database.

Integrating Database for Users

We introduce the **UserEntity** class and a **UserRepository**, where you can store username, encoded password, and role in the database. To create a custom **UserDetailsService** implementation which loads a **UserEntity** by username and converts it to a **UserDetails** instance, it must align with Spring Security's expectations. This service fetches the user's hashed password and roles from the database at login time. If the credentials match, authentication succeeds. Adopting a **PasswordEncoder** like bcrypt ensures that passwords are securely stored. When a user registers, encode the password before saving it to the database, preventing accidental exposure of plain-text credentials.

Adding Password Encoder

By default, storing plain-text passwords in a database is unsafe. A **PasswordEncoder** transforms plain-text passwords into hashed strings that cannot be easily reversed. Hashing means that if an attacker gains access to the database, they only see hashed values. Using **PasswordEncoderFactories.createDelegatingPasswordEncoder()** provides a modern approach, supporting algorithms like bcrypt. When the user logs in, Spring Security encodes the presented password and compares it with the stored hash. If both match, authentication succeeds. Failure to match means incorrect credentials.

Running Application and Testing

After configuring a security filter chain, user details service, and password encoder, testing the application reveals the results of the setup. Accessing a protected endpoint prompts for login. With the correct username and password, the user logs in successfully. A "USER" role might allow accessing some endpoints, while an "ADMIN" role unlocks others. If a user tries to access an endpoint without the proper role, Spring Security returns a 403 error. These standard HTTP responses and status codes help clients understand what went wrong—401 implies unauthenticated requests, and 403 implies unauthorized access.

If using a web-based login, Spring Security's default login page appears. Customizing this page involves specifying a login page URL in the security configuration. Similarly, a logout URL can facilitate session termination. If building a stateless REST API, consider using **httpBasic()** for testing, where clients send credentials with each request. For production APIs, a token or JWT-based approach might be preferred, eliminating the need for sessions or cookies and fitting better with mobile clients or single-page applications.

Handling Stateless Authentication with Tokens

Session-based authentication suits many scenarios, but microservices and stateless APIs often benefit from a token approach. Instead of maintaining a server-side session, the server issues a JWT or another form of token after successful login. The client stores this token and attaches it to each request. Spring Security can integrate a custom filter to parse and validate the token, load user details, and authenticate the request. This approach does not rely on cookies or server memory for sessions, scaling more easily across multiple instances. Although token-based authentication requires some custom logic (like writing a **JwtAuthenticationFilter**), it keeps the API stateless and simpler to scale horizontally.

Customizing Login and Logout

You can also improve the user experience by tweaking the login and logout flows. Instead of using the default login page, set a custom page, or for REST APIs, handle authentication at the API level. You can also customize failure handlers to return structured JSON responses when there's a login failure, which helps with client-side error handling. If roles and authorities need to appear in token payloads or session attributes, extend the logic to store these details. And for logout, make sure to specify a logout URL or implement a token revocation strategy. That way, when users log out, any requests tied to that token or session will be invalidated.

As things get more complicated, add features like password reset flows, account locking after repeated failed logins, or integration with external identity providers. And the good news is that Spring Security's architecture can handle all these additions without having to rework the core logic. For example, when you set up a password reset, it might send a token via email, and then verify it when the user requests it. Account locking might integrate with **UserDetails** properties to disable login attempts. External providers (OAuth2 or OpenID Connect) can replace local username/password schemes, delegating authentication to trusted identity services.

Testing and Maintenance

You should test your authentication flow regularly with integration tests. For example, a test that attempts to access a protected endpoint without the right credentials should expect a 401 response. Another test tries logging in with the right credentials and expects a 200 response. If roles matter, test endpoints that are only allowed to admins, making sure that requests from a "USER" role produce a 403. If your company uses token-based authentication, make sure you test token generation, token expiration, and invalid token handling. These tests make sure that your security configurations stay consistent and reliable even after code changes. And if performance's something you're concerned about, then you should probably check the overhead of repeatedly hashing passwords during logins. Usually, hashing happens just the once per login attempt, which is often acceptable. If your user databases get big, indexing by username and maybe caching user details might help performance. Since Spring Security is flexible, caching commonly requested user details can speed up authentication. Another strategy is to scale horizontally by using stateless tokens. Each instance can validate tokens independently without centralized session management.

For integration with frontend clients, we need to document login endpoints, say that clients need to provide credentials or tokens, and explain error responses. It's also good to explain that 401 means "login required" and 403 means "insufficient privileges" so frontend developers can handle user feedback gracefully. If a client fails to attach a valid token or uses expired credentials, the

API's consistent HTTP responses can help them re-authenticate or present the right credentials. If new roles show up, like "EDITOR" or "PUBLISHER," add them to the security logic. If certain endpoints get more sensitive over time, update the security configuration to require higher-level roles or authorities.

By following these steps and refining the details over time, authentication in the application remains secure, flexible, and aligned with evolving requirements. Users can confidently trust that their credentials stay safe, and the system ensures that only valid, authorized requests succeed.

Role-Based Access Control

Understanding Roles and Authorities

With the established authentication and basic authorization checks, expanding to a role-based access control model refines how we manage user permissions. Roles define categories of access within the system. Instead of assigning fine-grained permissions directly to each user, roles group together related authorities or privileges. Assigning roles to users simplifies maintenance. For example, an "ADMIN" role might include privileges like editing books, managing authors, and accessing administrative dashboards. A "USER" role might be limited to reading public data. By associating users with roles, the application enforces consistent access rules without individually configuring each permission.

Within the ambit of Spring Security, roles often appear as a high-level abstraction. Internally, these roles translate into granted authorities (like **ROLE_ADMIN** or **ROLE_USER**). The framework expects roles to be prefixed with "ROLE_" by default. Assigning the role "ADMIN" to a user results in a granted authority named "ROLE_ADMIN" for security checks. This design ensures a uniform approach and reduces confusion. If more granular control is needed, defining specific authorities beyond roles is possible. A role might represent a bundle of authorities, allowing the application to scale its authorization logic gracefully as it grows.

Defining Roles in User Store

The implementation of role-based access control starts at the data layer. Whether using an in-memory user store or a database-backed **UserDetailsService**, you must assign roles when creating user accounts.

Let us take an in-memory scenario:

```
UserDetails adminUser = User.builder()
    .username("admin")
    .password(passwordEncoder.encode("adminpass"))
```

```
    .roles("ADMIN") // This sets ROLE_ADMIN
    .build();
```

In a database-backed scenario, the **UserEntity** might have a **role** field that stores a string like "ADMIN" or "USER." When loading the user, the **UserDetailsService** translates this field into a **GrantedAuthority** named "ROLE_ADMIN" or "ROLE_USER." If multiple roles per user are needed, store them in a separate table or a list field. Each role that's retrieved corresponds to a specific authority. When you structure your data like this, changing a user's role doesn't mean you have to alter the code. All you have to do is update the database record.

Configuring Authorization Rules

After assigning the roles to users, specifying which endpoints require which roles is straightforward. The **HttpSecurity** configuration's **authorizeHttpRequests()** method provides a fluent DSL for expressing these rules. For instance:

```
http.authorizeHttpRequests(auth -> auth
    .antMatchers("/admin/**").hasRole("ADMIN")
    .antMatchers("/user/**").hasAnyRole("USER", "ADMIN")
    .antMatchers("/public/**").permitAll()
    .anyRequest().authenticated()
);
```

This above simple code enforces that any request to an **/admin** endpoint requires the "ADMIN" role, while **/user** endpoints accept either "USER" or "ADMIN" roles. This pattern centralizes authorization logic in one place, making policies easy to comprehend and modify. If requirements change—maybe "USER" roles lose access to certain endpoints—adjusting a single line in the configuration updates the system's behavior.

Method-Level Security

While HTTP endpoint restrictions are often sufficient, sometimes more granular control is required at the service or method level. Let us take for an example that there is a certain business logic that might only run if the caller has "ADMIN" privileges. Now here., adding Spring's method-level security allows us to annotate service methods with constraints like **@PreAuthorize("hasRole('ADMIN')")**. After enabling method-level security (e.g., **@EnableGlobalMethodSecurity(prePostEnabled = true)**), use annotations directly on methods:

```java
@PreAuthorize("hasRole('ADMIN')")
public void deleteBook(Long id) {
    // Only admins can delete books
    repository.deleteById(id);
}
```

If a user without the "ADMIN" role calls this method, the call fails before execution. This approach keeps authorization logic close to the relevant business logic. If endpoint-level restrictions are too coarse or if certain conditions depend on the current user, method-level security provides a flexible solution.

Evolving Roles and Permissions

As the application matures, new roles might emerge. Suppose we introduce a "PUBLISHER" role that can create and edit books but not manage authors. In that case, adding a new role and adjusting the authorization configuration suffices. Assign the "PUBLISHER" role to certain users and update endpoint mappings accordingly:

```java
.antMatchers("/books/create").hasAnyRole("ADMIN", "PUBLISHER")
.antMatchers("/authors/manage").hasRole("ADMIN")
```

If eventually we need more granular permissions, define custom authorities like "BOOK_WRITE" or "AUTHOR_DELETE." Assign these authorities to roles. The "ADMIN" role might include "BOOK_WRITE" and "AUTHOR_DELETE," while the "PUBLISHER" role only includes "BOOK_WRITE." In this scenario, method-level annotations can check for **`hasAuthority('BOOK_WRITE')`** instead of **`hasRole('ADMIN')`**, offering more precise control.

If the backend enforces roles and authorities, the frontend or client might adapt UI based on user roles. For instance, an admin dashboard might only appear if the authenticated user has the "ADMIN" role. The backend provides a way to retrieve current user roles (e.g., through a **`/me`** endpoint), enabling the client to conditionally render features. This approach provides a better user experience, showing only relevant options. The client may hide admin buttons if the user lacks "ADMIN" privileges, preventing confusion.

If performance or scalability concerns arise, consider caching user roles or authorities. Normally, roles do not change frequently. If users are stored in a database, load them once at login and store their granted authorities in memory or in a token for stateless scenarios. If complex logic determines roles dynamically, precomputing them could save CPU cycles at runtime. Balancing flexibility and performance depends on the application's scale and requirements.

By implementing role-based access control, we add a powerful layer of authorization to the application. This makes sure only people with the right permissions can perform actions. This keeps the system secure as it grows, and makes it easy to keep track of who can do what.

Summary

Overall, you got to learn how Spring Security is integrated into the application for authentication and authorization. You understood that authentication established who the user was, while authorization controlled what actions that user could perform. You learned to configure a security chain that restricted endpoints, and used user stores, either in-memory or database-backed, to verify credentials securely with password encoding. You also observed how establishing tokens or sessions allowed authenticated users to access protected resources.

Next, you saw how roles and authorities simplified managing permissions. You had defined roles like "USER" or "ADMIN" and mapped them to endpoints, ensuring only authorized individuals could perform sensitive actions. You had also utilized method-level security to enforce rules directly on service methods. Through testing and adjustments, you had confirmed that the security settings worked as intended. Ultimately, you had built a layered security model that provided a flexible, maintainable solution for controlling access and operations within the system.

CHAPTER 8: CACHING WITH REDIS

Understanding Caching Concepts

So far, whenever a client requests information—like a list of books or the details of a particular author—the backend queries the database. If the same data is requested frequently, repeatedly executing the same SQL queries can become expensive. Over time, as the application's load grows and the dataset expands, the constant round-trips to PostgreSQL add latency and consume valuable resources. Even when indexes optimize certain queries, repeatedly retrieving unchanged data still involves network I/O, CPU cycles, and memory overhead on the database server. This scenario invites a solution that can reduce these repetitive lookups. Caching addresses this issue by storing frequently accessed data in a faster storage medium. Instead of hitting the database every time, the application checks if the requested information is available in a cache. If present, returning the cached data avoids a database query entirely. The result is improved performance, reduced load on the database, and quicker response times for end-users. Caching effectively acts as a shortcut, remembering results for a certain period or until invalidation rules apply.

While some caching might be possible with memory-based solutions within the Java application itself, these often lack robustness, scalability, and distributed capabilities. If multiple application instances run behind a load balancer, relying on an in-memory cache per instance leads to inconsistent caches. One instance may have the cached data, another may not. To provide a more reliable and scalable caching layer, introducing an external cache store like Redis proves beneficial. Redis is an in-memory data structure store known for its speed, flexibility, and wide adoption. Redis stores data in memory, making read operations extremely fast. Unlike relational databases, Redis does not parse queries or manage complex joins every time you request data. Retrieving a value by key is a straightforward, O(1) time complexity operation in many cases. This dramatically reduces the time required to respond to client requests. If a user frequently requests the same piece of information, rather than repeating a database query, the backend returns the cached data from Redis almost instantaneously. The improvement becomes especially noticeable under high load or when accessing large datasets.

Caching also offloads work from the PostgreSQL database. By serving a portion of requests directly from Redis, the database can focus on operations that truly need fresh data or involve complex transactions. For instance, consider a scenario where the homepage displays a list of recently published books. Without caching, every homepage request triggers a SELECT query on PostgreSQL. With caching, the first request queries the database and stores the result in Redis. Subsequent requests hit Redis, returning the same result instantly until the cache expires or the underlying data changes. This decreases database CPU usage and reduces contention for database locks and resources. The key to effective caching lies in choosing what data to cache and when to invalidate it. While caching can speed up read operations, cached data might become stale if the underlying database changes. Designing an appropriate cache expiration strategy or implementing triggers that update or remove cache entries keeps data consistent. For example, if a book's price changes, the application might need to invalidate or update the cached entry. A common approach involves setting a Time-To-Live (TTL) on cached items, after which they expire automatically. Another approach involves programmatically removing or updating cache entries when changes occur in the database.

Redis supports a variety of data structures—strings, lists, sets, hashes, sorted sets—enabling flexible caching patterns. In a simple scenario, each cached entity might be stored as a JSON string keyed by a unique identifier. For example, a book record with ID 123 could be stored under the key **`book:123`**. Retrieving that book's details involves a single GET operation. For more complex queries, one might store entire result sets keyed by query parameters, or break down large datasets into manageable fragments. Redis's ability to store structured data and apply atomic operations on them helps maintain efficient and reliable caches.

The integration of Redis with Spring Boot and our existing codebase is straightforward. By adding dependencies and configuring connection details, the application can connect to a Redis server. Spring Data Redis, a Spring project dedicated to Redis integration, simplifies operations by providing templates and repository abstractions. Once set up, adding caching annotations like **`@Cacheable`**, **`@CachePut`**, and **`@CacheEvict`** on service methods automatically stores and retrieves data from Redis. For instance, annotating a method that fetches a book by ID with **`@Cacheable("books")`** ensures that the returned value is cached under a key derived from the method's parameters. On subsequent calls with the same ID, Spring checks the cache first.

While Redis is great for caching, it's also good for other things like messaging, pub/sub, distributed locks, and more. For us, focusing on caching improves performance and eases the load on PostgreSQL. As we move forward, we can try out different caching strategies, play around with TTL values, and make caching policies even better. When caching is set up right, it can speed things up a lot. Clients get responses faster, and backend services handle more requests without needing to scale up database resources. The system as a whole gets more efficient, users are happier, and operational costs might go down since the database isn't as stressed. But it's important to keep in mind that caching works best for data that doesn't change often or for results that are costly to compute.

If certain endpoints always return dynamic data or rarely benefit from repeated queries, caching might not help. So, it's important to spot these patterns and use caching in the right places. This keeps Redis from being a drain on resources. Some operations might be too unpredictable to benefit from caching, while others might see huge improvements by avoiding constant database hits. When you're dealing with production environments, it's good to put Redis on its own server, or use a service that manages it, to make sure it's always available and can handle a lot of requests. If your app runs in a cluster, Redis can be a centralized cache. All the nodes access and store data in Redis, so everything's consistent and there's less chance of a stale or uncached result. If the load increases, you can scale Redis vertically (with more memory or CPU) or horizontally (with cluster modes) to accommodate growth. And if you keep an eye on key metrics like memory usage, key eviction, and hit/miss ratios, you can make sure your caching strategy stays on track.

By introducing Redis into the stack, we acknowledge that not all queries deserve equal treatment. Some data rarely changes, and fetching it from PostgreSQL every time is wasteful. With Redis in place, the application can focus database resources on complex queries that genuinely require fresh, non-cached data. As a result, both average and peak response times improve. Under heavy load, these improvements become even more significant, preventing slowdowns or timeouts that harm user experience.

Integrating Redis with Spring Boot

Now, the next step involves setting up Redis and integrating it into the Spring Boot application. This process includes installing Redis, connecting the application to the Redis server, and configuring the necessary beans or templates to start using Redis as a cache backend.

First, make sure you've got a Redis server that's accessible. Putting Redis on your development machine is pretty simple. On Linux-based systems, package managers offer an **apt install redis-server** or similar commands to get Redis running. Docker simplifies the process as shown below:

```
docker run -d --name redis -p 6379:6379 redis
```

This command starts a Redis container listening on port 6379. Confirm Redis is running by connecting with the Redis CLI tool (**redis-cli**) and issuing a **ping** command, expecting a "PONG" response. With Redis now available, the application can connect to it. In our project, you then add the required dependencies for Redis integration. The **spring-data-redis** and **jedis** or **lettuce** client dependencies enable communication with Redis:

```
<dependency>
    <groupId>org.springframework.boot</groupId>
    <artifactId>spring-boot-starter-data-redis</artifactId>
</dependency>
```

This starter pulls in Spring Data Redis and a default client (Lettuce by default), simplifying configuration. Next, we then configure the connection properties in **application.properties** or **application.yml**:

```
spring.redis.host=localhost
spring.redis.port=6379
```

You then adjust these values as needed if the Redis server runs on another host or port. In a containerized environment, use Docker networking or environment variables to specify these details. Once the application starts, Spring Boot attempts to connect to Redis.

Next, to leverage caching, add caching support to the Spring Boot application. Enable caching by annotating a configuration class with **@EnableCaching**. For example:

```
import org.springframework.cache.annotation.EnableCaching;
import org.springframework.context.annotation.Configuration;
@Configuration
@EnableCaching
public class CacheConfig {
    // Additional cache-related beans can go here if needed
}
```

This annotation tells Spring that it should scan for caching annotations like **@Cacheable**, **@CachePut**, and **@CacheEvict** on beans and manage them using a cache manager. By default, Spring Boot detects the presence of Redis dependencies and configures a **RedisCacheManager** if possible. If customization is needed, define a **RedisCacheManager** bean. For a basic setup, relying on auto-configuration suffices.

Once caching is enabled, annotate service methods to use the cache. For example, if a **BookService** method retrieves a book by ID from the database, annotate it as follows:

```
import org.springframework.cache.annotation.Cacheable;
public class BookService {
    @Cacheable(value = "books", key = "#id")
    public Book getBookById(Long id) {
        return repository.findById(id).orElse(null);
    }
}
```

With **@Cacheable("books")**, the first time **getBookById** is called with a particular ID, it fetches the book from the database and stores it in Redis under a key derived from the **value** ("books") and **key** ("#id"). Subsequent calls with the same ID return the cached value, skipping the database. If the book changes, consider using **@CacheEvict** on methods that update the book to remove or invalidate the old cached entry.

To verify that caching works, run the application and call the endpoint associated with **getBookById** multiple times. Enable Redis command logs or use the **redis-cli** tool to observe keys created in Redis. After the first call, subsequent requests should hit Redis rather than the database. Performance improvements might be subtle in a development environment but become more apparent under load or when data retrieval is expensive.

For more advanced configurations, customize the cache manager. For instance, specifying TTLs ensures that cached entries expire after a certain period. A configuration might look like this:

```
import
org.springframework.data.redis.cache.RedisCacheConfiguration;
import java.time.Duration;
@Bean
public RedisCacheConfiguration cacheConfiguration() {
    return RedisCacheConfiguration.defaultCacheConfig()
        .entryTtl(Duration.ofMinutes(10))
        .disableCachingNullValues();
}
```

This sets a 10-minute TTL on cached items. After 10 minutes, Redis automatically removes them, ensuring that stale data does not linger indefinitely. If data changes more frequently, shorter TTLs keep the cache closer to reality. For less dynamic data, longer TTLs reduce database load more effectively.

In a production environment, consider using a managed Redis service or a high-availability setup. If running in the cloud, providers offer managed Redis instances that handle replication, failover, and scaling. Spring Data Redis integrates seamlessly with these setups, and the application only needs updated connection details. Monitoring Redis memory usage, eviction policies, and key hit/miss ratios ensures that the chosen caching strategy yields tangible benefits. If multiple caches or different caching policies are needed, define multiple **`@Cacheable`** value spaces or use **`@CacheConfig`** on classes to share cache properties. Mixing and matching caching strategies for different parts of the application allows tailoring caching policies to specific data patterns. Some endpoints might use short-lived caches, while others store results longer. By experimenting with these combinations, achieving an optimal balance of freshness and performance becomes easier.

Finally, remember that caching is a tool, not a silver bullet. If certain data is rarely requested or updated frequently, caching might not help. In some cases, caching could even introduce complexity by serving stale data if not invalidated properly. Start by caching read-heavy, rarely-changing data and measure performance improvements. Adjust caching coverage gradually, adding new caches or refining TTLs based on observed results in production. Over time, the integrated Redis caching layer can become a key component of a responsive and scalable system.

Implementing Caching

Identifying What to Cache

So, to integrate Redis caching into GitforGits, first you've got to figure out which parts of the application benefit the most from caching. You should think about endpoints that fetch data that's frequently requested and doesn't change often, like a list of recently published books, author profiles, or top-rated titles. These queries can be costly on PostgreSQL if you run them a bunch of times, so caching their results can reduce database load and speed up response times. But don't cache data that changes a lot or needs to be super fresh. It's best to start with stable, read-heavy endpoints as a solid starting point.

For instance, if **getBookById(Long id)** in **BookService** repeatedly queries the database for the same book, annotate it with **@Cacheable** to store the result in Redis. Future requests for the same ID return instantly from the cache until the entry expires or is evicted. Similarly, if an endpoint retrieves a list of all authors or featured books for the GitforGits homepage, caching the list reduces repeated database hits.

Applying Caching Annotations

With Redis configured and **@EnableCaching** active, adding caching to methods is straightforward. Suppose **BookService** has a method:

```
@Cacheable(value = "books", key = "#id")
public Book getBookById(Long id) {
    return bookRepository.findById(id).orElse(null);
}
```

The first time this method runs for a given **id**, it queries the database and caches the resulting **Book** object under a Redis key derived from "books::id". Subsequent calls for the same **id** hit the cache, bypassing the database. If **@Cacheable** seems insufficient or you need to refresh cached data after an update, use **@CacheEvict** or **@CachePut** on methods that modify the underlying data. For example, when a book's details change:

```
@CacheEvict(value = "books", key = "#book.id")
public Book updateBook(Book book) {
    // update in database
    return bookRepository.save(book);
}
```

This clears the cached entry for that book ID, ensuring that the next **getBookById** call fetches updated data from the database before re-caching it.

Choosing TTL Strategy

While caching accelerates reads, storing data indefinitely can lead to stale information. Setting a Time-To-Live (TTL) on cache entries ensures eventual refresh. A TTL of a few minutes or hours might strike a balance between performance and data freshness. For relatively static data, longer TTLs reduce database load. For rapidly changing data, shorter TTLs keep caches current.

If previously configured a **RedisCacheConfiguration** bean with a default TTL, all entries have that expiration by default. Adjusting TTLs might depend on the type of data. For a list of featured books (which might change daily), a TTL of 30 minutes suffices. For book details, which might remain stable for hours unless updated, a longer TTL is reasonable. Experimenting with TTLs and monitoring results helps fine-tune performance.

Handling Stale Data and Invalidation

No matter how carefully caching is implemented, certain events require immediate invalidation. If a user publishes a new edition of a book and the old edition's data remains in the cache, clients might receive outdated information. Using **@CacheEvict** on methods that write to the database ensures that stale entries vanish promptly. Another approach is calling **CacheManager** methods directly from code whenever certain conditions occur.

If the application triggers periodic updates (e.g., a scheduled task updates featured books hourly), consider programmatically evicting old entries. Redis supports atomic operations, so removing or updating keys is efficient. Consistency between cached data and the underlying database is a priority. While perfect consistency might be hard to achieve, well-placed evictions and short TTLs minimize discrepancies.

Caching Complex Queries and Result Sets

Beyond simple lookups by ID, consider caching more complex queries, like retrieving all books by a certain author or all titles matching certain criteria. Caching such queries can dramatically improve performance if clients repeatedly request them. Annotating these methods with **@Cacheable** works the same way, but choosing keys that reflect the query parameters is vital to avoid collisions.

Let us take an example:

```
@Cacheable(value = "booksByAuthor", key = "#authorName")
public List<Book> getBooksByAuthor(String authorName) {
    return bookRepository.findByAuthorName(authorName);
```

```
}
```

This stores the result under "booksByAuthor::authorName". Next calls for the same authorName load from the cache. If new books by that author appear, use **@CacheEvict** or a TTL to ensure that the list eventually reflects changes. One might also consider using more granular caching strategies, splitting large result sets into chunks or adopting patterns like a "book index" cache.

Monitoring and Adjusting Cache Usage

As caching takes effect, keep an eye on Redis metrics. Take a look at the hit/miss ratios: if there are a lot of hits, that means caching is saving database queries. If the miss ratio stays high, think about adjusting what's cached, expiration times, or keys. Also keep an eye on memory usage. Redis stores data in memory, so if you've got a big cache, you're using up a lot of RAM. If you're low on memory, use eviction policies (like LRU) to discard the least recently used keys. And Spring Data Redis lets you set those eviction policies at the cache level.

If certain queries don't benefit from caching or cause memory bloat, reconsider caching them. Also, caching isn't required for all endpoints. Just pick the most important or frequently used data to get the biggest impact. And as your load patterns change, it's a good idea to take another look at your caching decisions. And don't forget to do regular audits to keep your cache layer in sync with changing needs.

Integrate Caching into CI/CD and Tests

Treat caching like any other feature. Write tests that verify caching behavior. For example, call **getBookById** twice and ensure the database method is invoked only once. After updating a book, ensure that **@CacheEvict** works and that subsequent reads hit the database again.

In continuous integration (CI) pipelines, consider spinning up a test Redis instance (via Docker) to ensure caching works in automated tests. If that's complex, rely on mocking frameworks or profiles that disable caching in certain tests. The goal is confidence that caching does not break logic or introduce stale results. If done carefully, caching tests reduce the likelihood of production issues.

Scaling and Enhancing the Caching Strategy

Now that GitforGits is growing, we might need to scale up Redis. You can run Redis in a cluster or use a managed service to handle larger datasets. If different endpoints need different TTLs, you can define multiple caches or provide custom keys with separate configurations. If some data should never expire, consider setting a no TTL for that subset, but remember to evict or update entries when data changes.

Eventually, we might see more advanced caching patterns pop up. For example, pre-warming the cache on app startup ensures that important queries are in there before the user makes their first request. Scheduled tasks to refresh caches proactively reduce latency spikes. And combining caching with rate limiting or other performance measures helps keep the user experience smooth. You could also use Redis as a distributed lock server or pub/sub system to take things even further beyond basic key-value caching.

Summary

In short, you learned that repeatedly querying a PostgreSQL database for the same data is a waste of time and resources. You saw that caching offered a solution by storing the most frequently accessed results in a faster, in-memory store like Redis. You used Redis to ease your database's workload, which sped things up. Instead of running SQL queries every time, the application got the info it needed from memory.

You figured out how to integrate Redis with Spring Boot and enable caching annotations. You also configured TTLs to prevent stale data from lingering and used cache eviction methods to make sure that updates in the database were reflected in cached results. You also figured out how to selectively apply caching to read-heavy endpoints, improve hit ratios, and measure performance gains. You also know that planning, monitoring, and adjusting caching strategies keeps things consistent and running smoothly. Overall, when you integrated Redis caching into the GitforGits project, you got faster responses, reduced the database workload, and provided a more efficient and scalable environment as the application grew.

Chapter 9: Messaging with Apache Kafka

Setting up Kafka

It's clear that building a modern backend system involves more than simple request-response interactions. When multiple microservices or components share data in real time, an asynchronous messaging solution is essential for ensuring uninterrupted communication without blocking each other. Apache Kafka is the ideal solution for this, operating as a distributed streaming platform with unparalleled capacity to manage large volumes of messages. Instead of services directly calling one another, they publish messages to Kafka topics and consume messages from those topics at their own pace. This decoupling ensures that if one service experiences issues, other parts of the system can continue operating because messages persist in Kafka until consumed.

The Kafka architecture relies on clusters of brokers storing and replicating data across multiple nodes. Producers send messages to Kafka topics. These topics are organized into partitions for scalability. Consumers then read messages from these partitions, enabling parallel processing. The platform supports retention policies, meaning messages remain available for a certain time window or size threshold. This flexibility allows for replaying old messages or recovering from errors. By adopting Kafka, an application can seamlessly integrate new services into the data flow by simply having them produce or consume relevant topics.

Installing and Configuring Kafka

There are a few ways to set up Kafka. Some folks like to install it manually on a local machine, while others use Docker containers or a cloud-hosted solution. If you're just trying something out on your own computer, the official Apache Kafka distribution works just fine. For small-scale development and testing, getting the binaries from the Apache Kafka website and extracting them into a dedicated directory usually works fine. Just make sure you've got Java installed, since Kafka needs a JVM to run.

A typical manual installation starts by downloading a tar.gz file containing both Kafka and Apache ZooKeeper. ZooKeeper traditionally coordinates the Kafka cluster by handling broker metadata and leader election for partitions. Although newer versions of Kafka can run without an external ZooKeeper, many still use it for stability and familiarity. After unzipping or untarring the Kafka package, start ZooKeeper by running a script like:

```
bin/zookeeper-server-start.sh config/zookeeper.properties
```

Next, launch a Kafka broker:

```
bin/kafka-server-start.sh config/server.properties
```

If these processes run without errors, Kafka should be reachable on the configured ports (default 2181 for ZooKeeper, 9092 for Kafka). Create a topic to confirm everything is working:

```
bin/kafka-topics.sh --create --topic test-topic --bootstrap-server localhost:9092 --partitions 1 --replication-factor 1
```

Then, run a producer in one terminal and a consumer in another:

```
bin/kafka-console-producer.sh --topic test-topic --bootstrap-server localhost:9092

bin/kafka-console-consumer.sh --topic test-topic --bootstrap-server localhost:9092 --from-beginning
```

If you type messages in the producer terminal, they should show up in the consumer terminal. That means Kafka is working. Just keep in mind that this local setup, while it can give you some good ideas, isn't for production use. For a real setup, you'll want to use multiple brokers on separate machines or Docker containers for replication and fault tolerance.

Integrating Kafka with Docker

If you prefer running Kafka in containers, a popular approach involves Docker Compose. A simple docker-compose.yml might look like:

```
version: '3'
services:
  zookeeper:
    image: confluentinc/cp-zookeeper:latest
    environment:
      ZOOKEEPER_CLIENT_PORT: 2181
    ports:
      - "2181:2181"
  kafka:
    image: confluentinc/cp-kafka:latest
    depends_on:
      - zookeeper
    environment:
      KAFKA_BROKER_ID: 1
      KAFKA_ZOOKEEPER_CONNECT: zookeeper:2181
```

```
      KAFKA_ADVERTISED_LISTENERS: PLAINTEXT://localhost:9092
      KAFKA_OFFSETS_TOPIC_REPLICATION_FACTOR: 1
    ports:
      - "9092:9092"
```

After saving the file, run **docker-compose up -d** to bring up ZooKeeper and Kafka containers. This approach avoids manual installation steps, ensuring everything is reproducible and portable. The same test commands from above, adjusted for container addresses, verify that Kafka is alive.

Configuration Considerations and Tuning

The Kafka's default settings suffice for small projects, but advanced tuning may be necessary as throughput grows. For instance, adjusting the partition count on key topics can improve parallel consumption. If events from a certain topic must be processed quickly, raising partition counts helps spread the load across multiple consumer instances. The replication factor ensures data resilience, so for production setups, a replication factor of at least 3 is common. This means each message is stored on three brokers, surviving broker failures.

In addition, the storage and retention policies matter a lot. If you want to keep messages for a week, set **log.retention.hours=168**. If a certain topic retains data indefinitely, be aware of disk space usage. Kafka can store terabytes of data, but capacity planning remains essential for a stable cluster. There are monitoring metrics, such as consumer lag and broker disk usage, that helps detect bottlenecks. There are special tools like Prometheus exporters that can track how each consumer group processes messages. If a consumer cannot keep pace, lag grows, indicating that you might need more consumer instances or more powerful hardware.

Securing and Networking

In general and by default, the Kafka runs on plaintext ports. For an internal development environment, that might be fine. Production deployments typically secure Kafka by enabling TLS (SSL) for encrypted traffic, ensuring that data in transit is safe from eavesdroppers. Authenticating clients with SSL certificates or SASL mechanisms prevents unauthorized producers or consumers from sending or retrieving messages. Configuring these security features involves setting the relevant properties (e.g., **ssl.keystore.location**) in server.properties. The final configuration depends on your environment and security requirements. If microservices run in a private network or container orchestration environment, additional steps might route traffic through secure proxies or load balancers.

Now here, the exposure of Kafka to external networks, such as a public cloud environment, requires careful control of ports and authentication methods. Advertised listeners define the addresses that external clients use. Docker users often mention the host's IP address or domain in **KAFKA_ADVERTISED_LISTENERS**, so that containers know how to route traffic. If you notice connection errors about "Broker may not be available," it might mean the container's host is misconfigured, or the port is unreachable from the client's perspective.

Linking Kafka to App

Once Kafka is running, the application can produce and consume messages. For instance, GitforGits might send an event every time a new book is published, containing metadata about the title, author, and timestamps. Other microservices or modules can subscribe to this event, updating caches, sending notifications, or performing analytics. In a Spring Boot environment, adding the **spring-kafka** dependency provides convenient templates for producing and consuming messages. For example, a producer might rely on **KafkaTemplate<String, Book>** to send serialized book data to a **book-publication** topic.

A typical configuration in Spring Boot's **application.properties** could look like:

```
spring.kafka.bootstrap-servers=localhost:9092
spring.kafka.consumer.group-id=gitforgits-consumer
spring.kafka.consumer.auto-offset-reset=earliest
```

Then, a producer bean might be defined:

```
@Bean
public KafkaTemplate<String, Book>
kafkaTemplate(ProducerFactory<String, Book> producerFactory) {
    return new KafkaTemplate<>(producerFactory);
}
```

If you use Avro or JSON for serialization, ensure the corresponding serializers are configured. Finally, a consumer might use a **@KafkaListener** annotation on a method that processes incoming messages:

```
@KafkaListener(topics = "book-publication", groupId =
"gitforgits-consumer")
public void handleBookPublication(Book book) {
    // Do something when a new book is published
}
```

With Kafka in there, the GitforGits architecture can evolve into a more event-driven model.

Rather than services checking for changes or calling each other directly, they'll post events to Kafka, letting the other services react as needed. The result is that it's more decoupled and scalable.

Producing and Consuming Messages

Once you've installed and configured Apache Kafka, the next step is pretty much a no-brainer: you can start producing and consuming messages. Kafka uses a publisher-subscriber pattern, which means we have one or more producers writing messages to a topic, and one or more consumers reading those messages. You can divide topics into partitions to make it scalable, so you can consume them in parallel. Producers don't have to worry about who's consuming the data, and consumers don't have to worry about how the data is published. This separates the components of the system. The model can handle a high throughput by replicating data across brokers and distributing the load among many consumers.

Setting up Spring-Kafka Dependency

To integrate with Spring Boot, including the **spring-kafka** dependency simplifies the process of sending and receiving messages. For example, in the **pom.xml**:

```
<dependency>
  <groupId>org.springframework.kafka</groupId>
  <artifactId>spring-kafka</artifactId>
  <version>2.9.0</version> <!-- Or a compatible version -->
</dependency>
```

Next, make sure the Kafka bootstrap servers are defined in your **application.properties** or **application.yml**:

```
spring.kafka.bootstrap-servers=localhost:9092
spring.kafka.consumer.group-id=gitforgits-consumer
spring.kafka.consumer.auto-offset-reset=earliest
```

These above properties inform Spring Boot where to locate Kafka and how to configure consumer defaults. The **group-id** organizes consumers into a logical group for load balancing and offset tracking. Setting **auto-offset-reset=earliest** ensures that if no prior offset is available, the consumer starts from the earliest messages.

Creating a Kafka Producer

A producer sends data to a Kafka topic. By defining a **KafkaTemplate** bean, you gain a straightforward API for sending messages. For instance:

```
import org.springframework.context.annotation.Bean;
import org.springframework.context.annotation.Configuration;
import org.springframework.kafka.core.ProducerFactory;
import org.springframework.kafka.core.KafkaTemplate;
@Configuration
public class KafkaProducerConfig {
    @Bean
    public KafkaTemplate<String, String> kafkaTemplate(
            ProducerFactory<String, String> producerFactory) {
        return new KafkaTemplate<>(producerFactory);
    }
}
```

In the above program, a **ProducerFactory** typically uses default settings or ones you have customized. If you need to produce JSON, Avro, or other formats, you can configure serializers accordingly. Once the **KafkaTemplate** is available, injecting it into a service class allows sending messages:

```
@Service
public class BookPublisher {
    private final KafkaTemplate<String, String> kafkaTemplate;
    public BookPublisher(KafkaTemplate<String, String>
kafkaTemplate) {
        this.kafkaTemplate = kafkaTemplate;
    }
    public void publishNewBook(String title) {
        kafkaTemplate.send("books-topic", title);
    }
}
```

In the above sample code, a simple string is sent. For real scenarios, you might send JSON or an object, but the principle remains. The call to **kafkaTemplate.send("books-topic", title)** returns immediately, and Kafka handles the data asynchronously. If you wish to handle success or failure, you can attach callbacks or use the returned **ListenableFuture**.

Creating a Kafka Consumer

A consumer reads messages from a topic. Spring Kafka's **@KafkaListener** simplifies this. We can define a method in a service class with **@KafkaListener(topics = "books-topic")** which automatically subscribes to that topic.

Let us take an example:

```
@Service

public class BookSubscriber {

    @KafkaListener(topics = "books-topic", groupId =
"gitforgits-consumer")

    public void consumeBookTitle(String title) {

        System.out.println("Received book title: " + title);

        // Additional processing

    }

}
```

When a producer sends a message to **books-topic**, the **BookSubscriber** method is triggered with the message payload. The **groupId** here ensures that if multiple consumer instances run with the same group, they share the load. If different microservices or modules use separate groups, they each get all messages independently.

Handling Complex Data Formats

If a simple string is insufficient, consider using JSON or a custom serialization format. Adding the Spring Kafka JSON converter or specifying Avro schemas is typical for more structured data. For JSON, specifying:

```
spring.kafka.producer.value-
serializer=org.springframework.kafka.support.serializer.JsonSe
rializer
```

```
spring.kafka.consumer.value-
deserializer=org.springframework.kafka.support.serializer.Json
Deserializer

spring.kafka.consumer.properties.spring.json.trusted.packages=
*
```

enables automatic conversion of objects to and from JSON. Then, you can define:

```
public class BookEvent {
    private String title;
    private String author;
    // getters, setters, etc.
}
```

A producer might do **kafkaTemplate.send("books-topic", new BookEvent("Title", "Author"));** while a consumer method signs for a **BookEvent** parameter. This approach keeps the code strongly typed and avoids manual parsing. Avro or Protobuf might replace JSON if you want stronger schema enforcement or smaller payload sizes.

Observing Offsets and Consumer Groups

Kafka tracks how each consumer group processes messages through offsets. If a consumer reads 100 messages and then restarts, Kafka knows it can resume at offset 101. This mechanism also allows multiple consumers in a group to share a topic's partitions. One consumer might get partition 0, while another gets partition 1, for instance. Monitoring consumer lag—the difference between the highest offset in a partition and the last committed offset—indicates if consumers keep up with traffic. Tools like **kafka-consumer-groups.sh** or GUI-based dashboards show these metrics. If lag grows too large, adding more consumer instances or partitions can help.

Reliability and Error Handling

Spring Kafka offers different methods for acknowledging messages. By default, the consumer commits offset automatically after processing. If a message triggers an exception, you can configure error-handling strategies like retries, dead-letter topics, or manual offset control. For instance, using a **SeekToCurrentErrorHandler** might automatically reprocess failed messages after a delay or route them to an error topic. These patterns protect against message loss. Additionally, producers can use **acks=all** in their properties to ensure replicas confirm receipt before proceeding, increasing data durability at the expense of some performance.

Integrating Kafka into App

Once you've got the basic Kafka producer and consumer patterns down, think about how to integrate Kafka into the GitforGits application for real-world activities. One idea could be to publish an event when a new book is created, and then have another service or module consume that event to run notifications, analytics, or logs.

Defining Event Model

Suppose we want to publish details about a newly added book. A simple Java class might capture the event data:

```
public class BookEvent {
    private String title;
    private String author;
    private String isbn;
    private String status;
    public BookEvent() { }
    public BookEvent(String title, String author, String isbn,
String status) {
        this.title = title;
        this.author = author;
        this.isbn = isbn;
        this.status = status;
    }
    // getters and setters
}
```

Here, if JSON is suitable, configuring JSON serialization for Kafka ensures that producers and consumers can send and receive **BookEvent** objects directly. For instance, adjusting **application.properties**:**spring.kafka.producer.value-serializer=org.springframework.kafka.support.serializer.JsonSerializer**

```
spring.kafka.consumer.value-
deserializer=org.springframework.kafka.support.serializer.Json
Deserializer

spring.kafka.consumer.properties.spring.json.trusted.packages=
*
```

This instructs Spring Kafka to convert **BookEvent** objects to and from JSON without manual coding.

Publishing a BookEvent

When a user adds a new book in the GitforGits platform, we can produce a **BookEvent** to a designated topic. For instance, define a **BookService** that saves a new book to the database, then publishes the event:

```
@Service

public class BookService {

    private final BookRepository bookRepository;

    private final KafkaTemplate<String, BookEvent>
kafkaTemplate;

    @Value("${gitforgits.kafka.topics.book-events}")

    private String bookEventsTopic;

    public BookService(BookRepository bookRepository,

                       KafkaTemplate<String, BookEvent>
kafkaTemplate) {

        this.bookRepository = bookRepository;

        this.kafkaTemplate = kafkaTemplate;

    }

    public Book createBook(String title, String author, String
isbn) {

        Book book = new Book(title, author, isbn, "DRAFT");

        bookRepository.save(book);

        // Publish event

        BookEvent event = new BookEvent(title, author, isbn,
"DRAFT");
```

```
        kafkaTemplate.send(bookEventsTopic, event);
        return book;
    }
}
```

In the above code snippet, the method saves the book to PostgreSQL, then constructs a **BookEvent** containing relevant details. The **kafkaTemplate.send(...)** call asynchronously sends the event to the configured **book-events** topic. If needed, add callbacks to handle send failures or success logs.

Consuming the Event

A consumer, possibly a separate module or microservice, listens for **BookEvent** messages. Let us take an example:

```
@Service
public class BookEventListener {
    @KafkaListener(topics = "#{${gitforgits.kafka.topics.book-events}}",
                   groupId = "gitforgits-consumer-group")
    public void onBookEvent(BookEvent event) {
        System.out.println("Received event: " + event.getTitle() + " by " + event.getAuthor());
        // Handle event logic
        // e.g., send notification, log status, or update search index
    }
}
```

The **@KafkaListener** annotation designates that **onBookEvent** subscribes to the **book-events** topic. The **groupId** ensures that multiple instances share the workload if scaled horizontally. If the consumer code resides in the same application, it automatically triggers. If in a separate microservice, a similar configuration can point to the same Kafka cluster and topic.

Logging and Auditing with Kafka

Besides direct business logic, Kafka can handle auditing or logging. For instance, define a separate producer call whenever a user modifies book metadata:

```
public void logBookUpdate(String userId, Book book) {
    BookEvent event = new BookEvent(book.getTitle(),
book.getAuthor(),

                                    book.getIsbn(),
book.getStatus());
    // Possibly add userId or timestamp fields to the event
    kafkaTemplate.send("book-update-logs", event);
}
```

A dedicated consumer or microservice might persist these logs to a data warehouse for analytics, or display them in real-time on an admin dashboard. This approach reduces coupling since logging is no longer buried inside the main code. If future analytics requires more detail, expand the event fields or parse them in the consumer.

Handling Errors and Retries

Production systems often face partial failures: a consumer might temporarily fail while processing messages, or the data might arrive malformed. Spring Kafka's container properties or error handler configurations let you set retry policies or direct messages to a dead-letter topic. For instance, specifying:

```
spring.kafka.listener.ack-mode=RECORD
spring.kafka.listener.concurrency=3
```

could let you process messages concurrently, acknowledging each record individually. For error handling, you might define a **SeekToCurrentErrorHandler** to retry a few times before discarding or moving the message to another topic. This ensures that transient failures do not lose data permanently, yet prevents endless loops for permanent errors.

Summary

So, you've got the hang of using Apache Kafka to decouple services in your backend, which lets you communicate asynchronously through message topics. You started by installing and configuring Kafka, either manually or via containers, then defined producers and consumers for sending and receiving messages. You figured out that topics and partitions let you handle a lot of messages at once and tolerate problems, so you could deal with big event streams without a hitch.

You've used Kafka integration in the GitforGits application to create events like new book additions or changes in publication status, and then used those for tasks like logging, notifications, or analytics. You realized that this event-driven approach made it easy to add new features without having to change any code. This chapter has shown you how to manage, tune, and observe Kafka-based messaging, making sure that GitforGits can handle any growth in the future.

CHAPTER 10: MICROSERVICES ARCHITECTURE WITH SPRING CLOUD

Spring Cloud Overview

Moving from one big program to a bunch of smaller ones is a lot more complicated than just dividing the code into different modules. We also handle challenges like service discovery, load balancing, configuration management, and routing. Spring Cloud has a bunch of tools that help with all of this, making it easier to create and maintain microservices. Instead of re-engineering each microservice separately, using Spring Cloud's prebuilt components saves effort and makes sure everything works the same way across the distributed system. In short, Spring Cloud helps you design, deploy, and scale smaller, independent services that, when put together, form a bigger application.

Why Microservices?

A monolithic application may become unwieldy as it grows, with new features making it harder to maintain, test, or deploy. Microservices aim to break functionality into smaller, loosely coupled services. Each service tackles a specific domain responsibility, which can evolve, scale, and deploy independently. If one service experiences higher load—say, a media service handling large file uploads—only that piece scales, reducing resource consumption and risk to other services. The application remains flexible, letting teams iterate quickly, adopt newer technologies, or fix bugs without risking the entire system. However, microservices bring complexity in the form of networking, cross-service communication, and distributed tracing. Spring Cloud addresses these complexities by providing consistent frameworks and patterns.

Key Components of Spring Cloud

Eureka for Service Discovery

When multiple services run in separate processes, each needs a way to locate others, especially if instances start and stop dynamically under a cloud or container environment. Eureka, a service discovery server, registers each microservice on startup and tracks the instances' health. Other services query Eureka to discover available service endpoints instead of relying on fixed hostnames or IP addresses. This approach ensures that if a service instance fails, Eureka removes it from the registry. Healthy instances remain discoverable, allowing clients or gateways to route requests properly.

For example, a **`BookService`** might register itself with Eureka as "BOOK-SERVICE." If the system scales out to three instances, Eureka tracks them. A **`SearchService`** that needs to call "BOOK-SERVICE" consults Eureka, obtains an available instance, and sends the request. This auto-registration and discovery pattern frees developers from hardcoding addresses. It also enables load balancing, since each request can choose a healthy instance. By pairing Eureka with Netflix Ribbon or Spring Cloud LoadBalancer, distributing traffic across instances becomes straightforward.

Zuul for API Gateway

It's tricky for outside clients or frontends to find individual microservices because they can spread out across a bunch of endpoints. An API gateway like Zuul or the newer Spring Cloud Gateway routes external traffic to the right microservice behind the scenes. Instead of having each service's direct URL, clients go through the gateway, and the gateway forwards requests to the right service. This setup makes security, rate limiting, logging, and other concerns easier to manage because they're all handled in one place instead of repeating them in each microservice.

Zuul from the Netflix OSS stack is pretty popular, but newer projects tend to go for Spring Cloud Gateway, which has a more modern reactive foundation. Either way, the gateway gets the service locations from Eureka, so it automatically adapts if new instances appear or vanish. The end result is a single entry point for external traffic, a consistent interface for external consumers, and a central place to enforce policies. Instead of changing client code whenever a service moves or scales, the gateway configuration updates automatically.

Config Server for Externalized Configuration

Microservices frequently require configuration data—like database credentials, feature flags, or environment details. Hardcoding these in the code leads to repeated deployments whenever settings change. The Spring Cloud Config Server provides a way to store configuration in a centralized repository (commonly Git), from which all microservices can fetch at runtime. Each service reads configuration keyed by profile or environment, letting us maintain separate settings for development, staging, or production without changing the code.

When a microservice starts, it contacts the Config Server for application-specific properties. If a property changes in the Git repo, you can refresh it without redeploying the service. For example, if the **`BookService`** needs a different cache size in production, you update a config file in the Git repo. The service automatically re-reads the property upon refresh. This pattern helps standardize environment management, remove sensitive credentials from code, and keep configuration under version control.

Benefits of Integrated Microservices

By combining service discovery (Eureka), an API gateway (Zuul or Spring Cloud Gateway), and centralized configuration (Config Server), the system gains structure. Each microservice focuses on business logic, registering itself with Eureka and pulling settings from the Config Server. External requests pass through the gateway. Additional features like circuit breakers (via Resilience4j or Hystrix) can protect from cascading failures. Observability tools like Spring Cloud Sleuth and Zipkin provide distributed tracing across multiple services. This integrated approach means when you create a new microservice—say, an **`AuthorService`**—the steps remain consistent. The service registers with Eureka, obtains its config from the Config Server, and optionally updates the gateway to route external calls from **`/authors/**`** to that service. Clients see only the gateway address, not multiple service addresses. The system remains flexible:

if the **AuthorService** scales to five instances or moves to another cluster node, Eureka and the gateway handle it automatically.

Imagine we have three microservices in GitforGits: **BookService**, **AuthorService**, and **SearchService**. Each runs in a container or a separate VM. On startup, each service registers with Eureka under its service name. Eureka maintains a registry listing all instances: **BOOK-SERVICE**, **AUTHOR-SERVICE**, **SEARCH-SERVICE**, each with one or more endpoints. The Config Server provides environment-specific properties for each. For instance, the search microservice might enable advanced indexing in production but not in development. A user's request arrives at the gateway with a path like **/books/123**. The gateway checks its routing rules, sees that **/books/**** belongs to **BOOK-SERVICE**, consults Eureka to pick a healthy instance, and forwards the request. The **BookService** might internally call **AuthorService** to fetch author details, again using Eureka for service discovery. That call remains internal and does not go back through the gateway. If **BookService** or **AuthorService** is currently scaling up, Eureka's updated registry ensures the traffic goes to newly spun-up instances when they're ready.

Though Spring Cloud eases microservices development, planning remains vital. A microservices architecture can be more complex to operate, as you handle network calls instead of local method calls. Monitoring, logging, and distributed tracing become essential to debug cross-service issues. Each service must handle partial outages gracefully—if **AuthorService** is down, **BookService** might display partial results. Patterns like circuit breakers or fallback methods help ensure resilience. The environment also must be robust, ideally employing Docker or Kubernetes to orchestrate services, scale them, and handle rolling updates.

The security aspect is also another key factor. Each microservice might need to authenticate requests or pass user tokens. The gateway can handle authentication, passing user context to downstream services. Alternatively, each service might require direct credentials, using an OAuth2 approach with tokens, or rely on advanced solutions like Spring Cloud Security or Keycloak integration. The Config Server might store secrets encrypted, requiring a secure method to decrypt them in production. The more microservices you have, the more crucial it becomes to standardize security processes.

The upcoming sections delves deeper into setting up a Config Server, registering microservices with Eureka, and configuring a gateway service. Each piece is essential for a fully functioning microservices environment, ensuring that new services integrate seamlessly. The result is a system that can scale horizontally, adopt new features quickly, and remain agile as the domain grows in size or complexity.

Setting up a Config Server

Purpose of a Config Server

A distributed system requires consistent, externalized configuration management to avoid scattering environment-specific properties across multiple services. A Config Server centralizes these properties and supplies them to individual microservices at runtime. Each service, when it starts, contacts the Config Server to retrieve its relevant settings, such as database credentials, message broker URLs, or feature flags. This strategy eliminates duplication across microservices and reduces the risk of mismatched configuration in your system.

The Config Server also accommodates dynamic refreshes. If a property changes in the configuration repository, you can notify the service to reload it on the fly. While not every property is suitable for live reloading, those that are can be adjusted with minimal disruption, saving time and increasing your system's agility. This ensures that secrets remain outside the codebase, where they can be managed securely and updated without code changes.

Creating a Config Server

We start by setting up a new Spring Boot project dedicated to the Config Server. Name it something like "config-server." In the **pom.xml**, add the Spring Cloud Config Server dependency. For example:

```
<dependencies>
    <dependency>
        <groupId>org.springframework.cloud</groupId>
        <artifactId>spring-cloud-config-server</artifactId>
        <version>3.1.5</version>
    </dependency>
    <!-- additional dependencies if needed -->
</dependencies>
```

Match the Spring Cloud version to your chosen Spring Boot version to maintain compatibility. Then, in the main application class annotated with **@SpringBootApplication**, add **@EnableConfigServer**:

```
@SpringBootApplication
@EnableConfigServer
public class ConfigServerApplication {
    public static void main(String[] args) {
        SpringApplication.run(ConfigServerApplication.class,
args);
```

```
    }
}
```

This annotation signals that the application is a Config Server, ready to respond to requests from microservices. Once you complete these steps, you have a basic Config Server that can run but still needs a backing store.

Connecting to a Configuration Repository

The Config Server expects to read files from a Git repository (commonly used) or another backend like SVN, file system, or Vault for secrets management. Assuming we rely on Git, we create a new repository that holds configuration files for your microservices. For instance, you might have a directory structure like:

```
config-repo/
  application.yml
  book-service.yml
  author-service.yml
  ...
```

In **application.yml**, you define global properties that all services can read. In **book-service.yml**, you specify properties only relevant to the BookService. Each file might hold multiple environment profiles such as **book-service-dev.yml** or **book-service-prod.yml**. Once pushed to a remote Git host, the Config Server can access it.

Next, point the Config Server to this Git repo by editing **application.properties** or **application.yml** in the Config Server project:

```
spring:
  cloud:
    config:
      server:
        git:
          uri: https://github.com/YourOrg/config-repo.git
          clone-on-start: true
```

When the Config Server starts, it clones or pulls the repository. If you want to store sensitive data, consider private Git repositories or use encryption. If credentials are needed, specify them in the properties, or rely on environment variables.

Running the Config Server and Testing

After setting these properties, run the Config Server. The console should show logs indicating it has cloned the Git repository successfully. To confirm that it serves configuration, point a browser or tool like **curl** to an endpoint like:

```
http://localhost:8888/book-service/default
```

In the above, **book-service** is the application name, and **default** is the profile. If a file named **book-service.yml** exists in the repo, you see the merged properties returned in JSON. If you specify a profile, such as **book-service-dev.yml**, you add **/book-service/dev**. This confirms that each microservice can request environment-specific files, falling back to global settings.

Integrating Microservices with the Config Server

Microservices that rely on the Config Server typically include the Spring Cloud Config Client dependency in their **pom.xml**:

```
<dependency>
    <groupId>org.springframework.cloud</groupId>
    <artifactId>spring-cloud-starter-config</artifactId>
    <version>3.1.5</version>
</dependency>
```

In their **bootstrap.yml** or **bootstrap.properties**, set the Config Server's address:

```
spring:
  application:
    name: book-service
  cloud:
    config:
      uri: http://localhost:8888
```

The microservice's name matches what you used in the config repo filenames, letting it pull the right files. On startup, the microservice contacts the Config Server at **`http://localhost:8888/book-service/default`** (or other profile) for properties. If it finds environment-specific configurations, those override the defaults. By loading properties during the bootstrap phase, these values become available before the main application context initializes, ensuring that essential settings like data source URLs are in place.

Handling Environment Profiles and Overrides

A typical microservice might define multiple profiles: **`dev`**, **`staging`**, and **`prod`**. If the microservice is launched with **`--spring.profiles.active=dev`**, it requests **`book-service-dev.yml`** from the Config Server. To further refine, you can keep secrets like passwords in an encrypted format. The Config Server can decrypt them if you configure encryption and provide a master key.

When changes occur in the Git repo, you can either restart the service or call a refresh endpoint if you add **`spring-boot-starter-actuator`** and set **`management.endpoints.web.exposure.include=refresh`**. Then a POST call to **`/actuator/refresh`** triggers the microservice to reload updated configuration. Some properties might need a restart if they cannot be dynamically refreshed. Others, like feature toggles or certain application-level flags, can be toggled on the fly.

Now here when a microservice depends on the Config Server, you may consider the following guidelines:

- If the Config Server cannot reach Git due to network issues, the server uses the last known good clone. Avoid single points of failure by replicating the Git repo or using a high-availability approach.
- You can tag config changes or link them to specific application versions. This ensures that rolling back code changes also reverts the configuration to a known state.
- If you host the config repo privately, store credentials securely. Limit who can push changes to the config repo. Potentially add encryption for secrets, so they remain protected at rest.
- Standardizing naming conventions for property files helps keep them organized. For instance, **`application.yml`** for global defaults, then **`[service-name].yml`** for service-specific configs, **`[service-name]-dev.yml`** for the dev profile, etc.
- Logging a summary of loaded properties when a microservice boots helps track which environment or profile is used. Also, the Config Server logs can confirm successful file retrieval.

This whole step completes a key component of the microservices architecture, harmonizing how services adapt to different environments without code duplication or manual editing across services.

Registering Microservices with Eureka

Role of Eureka

It's important to have a solid way to find services in distributed systems. Microservices often create multiple instances on dynamic hosts or containers, so it's not practical to rely on static IPs or hostnames. Eureka is a service discovery server from Netflix OSS that solves this by maintaining a registry of running instances, which should help a lot. Each microservice registers itself on startup. Eureka keeps an eye on the instances to make sure they're running well, and if one goes down, it takes care of removing it. Other services check in with Eureka when they need to call a specific service, so developers don't have to hardcode addresses.

Typically, you'll have one or more Eureka servers. Each microservice runs an embedded Eureka client that automatically registers. If a microservice's instance count changes, Eureka's registry updates. Other services can query Eureka or integrate with load balancing libraries like Ribbon to spread requests across healthy instances. This way, services don't depend on the physical network setup. Instead of using "book-service:8081," a microservice calls "BOOK-SERVICE," and Eureka supplies the real endpoint.

Installing a Eureka Server

Now here to create a dedicated Eureka server, one has to often follow a pattern similar to a Config Server. The Spring Boot application is set up with the Spring Cloud Netflix Eureka Server dependency.

Here, in the **`pom.xml`**:

```
<dependencies>
    <dependency>
        <groupId>org.springframework.cloud</groupId>
        <artifactId>spring-cloud-starter-netflix-eureka-server</artifactId>
        <version>3.1.5</version>
    </dependency>
    <!-- other dependencies -->
</dependencies>
```

Then, in the main class:

```
@SpringBootApplication
```

```
@EnableEurekaServer
public class EurekaServerApplication {
    public static void main(String[] args) {
        SpringApplication.run(EurekaServerApplication.class,
args);
    }
}
```

The **@EnableEurekaServer** annotation activates the Eureka server features. A typical **application.properties** includes:

```
server.port=8761
eureka.client.register-with-eureka=false
eureka.client.fetch-registry=false
```

These settings indicate a standalone server that does not attempt to register with itself. Running this application starts a Eureka console at **http://localhost:8761**, showing a dashboard that eventually lists registered services.

For a production setup, consider multiple Eureka servers in a cluster to avoid a single point of failure. Each server replicates the registry among peers. Instances could run in different availability zones, ensuring that the registry remains accessible if one server goes offline. DNS or load balancer entries might point services to any of these Eureka servers.

Registering the Microservices

Next, once the Eureka server is operational, each microservice includes the Spring Cloud Netflix Eureka Client dependency:

```
<dependency>
    <groupId>org.springframework.cloud</groupId>
    <artifactId>spring-cloud-starter-netflix-eureka-
client</artifactId>
    <version>3.1.5</version>
</dependency>
```

In **application.yml**, a microservice might specify:

```
spring:
  application:
    name: book-service
eureka:
  client:
    serviceUrl:
      defaultZone: http://localhost:8761/eureka/
  instance:
    preferIpAddress: true
```

In the above, when the application starts, it contacts **`http://localhost:8761/eureka/`** to register itself under the name "book-service." Eureka shows the instance on its dashboard. The property **`preferIpAddress`** or **`hostname`** can be used to control how the service advertises its address. If multiple replicas run, each one registers under the same name with a unique instance ID. Eureka monitors health using heartbeats. If a microservice stops sending them, Eureka eventually marks it as offline and removes it from the registry.

Services that you want to call "book-service" use the name "BOOK-SERVICE" in discovery. For instance, if a "search-service" needs to find "book-service," it calls **`LoadBalancerClient`** or uses a client library that queries Eureka. It removes the need to embed IP addresses or ports in the code. If "book-service" scales from one to three instances, the searching code sees all of them, distributing requests automatically.

Configuring a Gateway Service

Need of Gateway

A microservice can spread quickly, and each one has its own endpoint or path. It can be a lot for outside clients to deal with, having to manage separate URLs, ports, or protocols for each service. An API gateway puts all that external access under one roof. The gateway routes incoming requests to the right service, handles cross-cutting concerns like authentication, rate limiting, or logging, and supplies a unified entry point. This setup hides internal details, so if a service changes its location, the gateway logic updates while client code stays the same.

It also integrates with Eureka. Instead of mapping routes statically, it queries the registry to find service addresses. It can also apply load balancing or failover policies. If certain services are offline, the gateway quickly detects and returns an error or fallback. This pattern makes things more resilient and maintainable. Plus, microservices can scale or switch hosts without any problems because clients always see a solid facade.

Setting up Spring Cloud Gateway

Historically, Zuul from Netflix was popular. Spring Cloud Gateway is the newer, more modern option. Both serve as an API gateway layer, but Spring Cloud Gateway offers a reactive foundation. For demonstration, consider using Spring Cloud Gateway.

For example, a new Spring Boot project might have:

```
<dependency>
    <groupId>org.springframework.cloud</groupId>
    <artifactId>spring-cloud-starter-gateway</artifactId>
    <version>3.1.5</version>
</dependency>
<dependency>
    <groupId>org.springframework.cloud</groupId>
    <artifactId>spring-cloud-starter-netflix-eureka-
client</artifactId>
    <version>3.1.5</version>
</dependency>
```

Then, a main class with **`@EnableDiscoveryClient`** if you want the gateway itself to register with Eureka:

```
@SpringBootApplication
@EnableDiscoveryClient
public class ApiGatewayApplication {
    public static void main(String[] args) {
        SpringApplication.run(ApiGatewayApplication.class,
args);
    }
}
```

Configuring Routes

A common pattern is to define routes in **application.yml**, telling the gateway how to map incoming paths to specific services:

```
spring:
  cloud:
    gateway:
      discovery:
        locator:
          enabled: true
```

When **discovery.locator.enabled** is true, the gateway automatically creates routes for each service in Eureka. Each service named "book-service" or "author-service" is accessible via a default path convention. For instance, "book-service" might appear under **/BOOK-SERVICE/****. If you prefer manual route definitions:

```
spring:
  cloud:
    gateway:
      routes:
        - id: book-service
          uri: lb://book-service
          predicates:
            - Path=/books/**
```

This means any request to **/books/**** is routed to the "book-service," using load balancing (the **lb://** prefix indicates a load-balanced address). The gateway consults Eureka for available instances. Additional filters might modify headers, enable security checks, or inject correlation IDs. For instance, you can define **filters** in the route or use global filters for logging. With this approach, clients or UI frontends just call **http://gateway-host/books/123**, and the gateway proxies that to the correct instance of the book-service.

Testing and Observability

The testing of a gateway usually involves spinning up the microservices, registering them with Eureka, and verifying that the gateway routes traffic properly. If the gateway is auto-generating routes from Eureka, confirm that each service appears as expected. Logs can reveal any mismatch or path collision. Also, the monitoring of metrics or distributed tracing (with Spring Cloud Sleuth and Zipkin) helps track requests from the gateway through each microservice, aiding debugging in complex flows.

If the gateway experiences high traffic, scaling horizontally is feasible. Each gateway instance still references Eureka to find service instances. Load balancers or container orchestrators can route external traffic to multiple gateway replicas. This approach ensures that if one gateway node fails, another continues to provide service. If we combine with multiple Eureka nodes, an environment emerges where each piece is designed to handle failures gracefully.

Summary

To sum it up, we learned that microservices need a cohesive approach for handling configuration, service discovery, and API routing. You created a Config Server to centralize properties, allowing each microservice to retrieve environment-specific settings from a version-controlled repository. You also introduced Eureka for dynamic service discovery. Each microservice registered itself with Eureka, eliminating the need for hardcoded addresses. This pattern lets you add or remove microservices without having to change the code, which makes it easier to add or remove microservices and deal with any problems.

Meanwhile, using an API gateway, you learned to manage all the traffic coming in from outside. The gateway's routes and filters took care of all the common problems, so the microservices could focus on their own jobs. All these tools from Spring Cloud worked together to create a flexible foundation for small services that could be used on their own. You also looked at how to use Spring Cloud Netflix Eureka to register services and how to build a gateway with Spring Cloud Gateway. Each microservice is integrated with the Config Server and retrieves environment properties on startup.These patterns make it easier to introduce new services or change existing ones.

Chapter 11: Testing and Debugging Backend Applications

Unit Testing with JUnit and Mockito

Building a reliable backend means verifying that individual components function correctly, and diagnosing failures when something goes wrong. Effective testing and debugging strategies cover multiple layers of the system, from low-level unit tests to integration and end-to-end scenarios. Early detection of code defects prevents cascading failures in production, while thorough debugging tools save time when diagnosing issues. To start, exploring unit testing with JUnit and Mockito ensures each class or method behaves as intended under controlled conditions.

Why Unit Testing?

A unit test focuses on the smallest piece of code—often a single method or class—verifying its correctness in isolation. By mocking dependencies, you avoid external complexities like databases or network calls, so a test can run quickly and deterministically. If all unit tests pass consistently, you gain confidence that the building blocks of your application are sound. Teams often integrate unit tests into CI pipelines, rejecting code merges that break existing tests.

JUnit, a popular Java testing framework, provides annotations like **`@Test`** for marking test methods, **`@BeforeEach`** for setup logic, and **`@AfterEach`** for teardown. Mockito, a mocking library, complements JUnit by replacing real dependencies with mocks or stubs. This ensures that classes under test do not inadvertently open connections, read files, or depend on complex external states. If your code references a repository or external service, Mockito intercepts calls to those dependencies and returns controlled outputs. This technique isolates the code path under scrutiny.

Installing JUnit and Mockito

If the application is a Maven-based project, include dependencies in **`pom.xml`**:

```
<dependency>
    <groupId>org.junit.jupiter</groupId>
    <artifactId>junit-jupiter</artifactId>
    <version>5.8.2</version>
    <scope>test</scope>
</dependency>
<dependency>
    <groupId>org.mockito</groupId>
    <artifactId>mockito-core</artifactId>
```

```
    <version>4.5.1</version>
    <scope>test</scope>
</dependency>
```

JUnit Jupiter is the latest iteration, offering modern annotations and improved extensibility. Mockito 4+ provides advanced mocking features. By scoping these dependencies to **test**, they do not affect production builds. Additionally, consider the **spring-boot-starter-test** dependency if using Spring Boot:

```
<dependency>
    <groupId>org.springframework.boot</groupId>
    <artifactId>spring-boot-starter-test</artifactId>
    <scope>test</scope>
</dependency>
```

This bundle includes JUnit, Mockito, and other libraries like AssertJ for fluent assertions. Once these dependencies are present, the test framework automatically scans for tests in the **src/test/java** directory.

Writing a Simple JUnit Test

Let us consider a simple service class as below:

```
@Service
public class CalculatorService {
    public int add(int a, int b) {
        return a + b;
    }
    public int multiply(int a, int b) {
        return a * b;
    }
}
```

Also, a JUnit 5 test might look like this:

```
class CalculatorServiceTest {
```

```
    private CalculatorService calculator;
    @BeforeEach
    void setup() {
        calculator = new CalculatorService();
    }
    @Test
    void testAdd() {
        int result = calculator.add(2, 3);
        Assertions.assertEquals(5, result);
    }
    @Test
    void testMultiply() {
        int result = calculator.multiply(4, 5);
        Assertions.assertEquals(20, result);
    }
}
```

Here, the **@BeforeEach** method ensures a fresh **CalculatorService** instance per test. Each **@Test** method checks a single scenario. If an assertion fails, JUnit flags it, marking the test as failed. A test class can have multiple test methods, each verifying a unique aspect or edge case. For instance, you might add negative numbers or zero-based checks. By default, running **mvn test** or the IDE's test runner executes these tests automatically.

Using Mockito to Mock Dependencies

When a class depends on other components—like a repository or external API—unit tests might become unwieldy if forced to set up real environments. The Mockito addresses this by mocking or stubbing those dependencies. Suppose a **BookService** interacts with a **BookRepository**. Instead of connecting to a real database, you create a mock repository that returns predefined data. For example:

```
@Service
public class BookService {
    private final BookRepository repository;
```

```
    public BookService(BookRepository repository) {
        this.repository = repository;
    }
    public Book findBookById(Long id) {
        return repository.findById(id).orElse(null);
    }
    // other methods
}
```

A test might look like:

```
@ExtendWith(MockitoExtension.class)
class BookServiceTest {
    @Mock
    private BookRepository repository;
    @InjectMocks
    private BookService bookService;
    @Test
    void testFindBookById_BookExists() {
        Book mockBook = new Book("Title", "Author");

when(repository.findById(1L)).thenReturn(Optional.of(mockBook)
);
        Book result = bookService.findBookById(1L);
        Assertions.assertNotNull(result);
        Assertions.assertEquals("Title", result.getTitle());
        Assertions.assertEquals("Author", result.getAuthor());
    }
    @Test
    void testFindBookById_NotFound() {
```

```
when(repository.findById(2L)).thenReturn(Optional.empty());
        Book result = bookService.findBookById(2L);
        Assertions.assertNull(result);
    }
}
```

The annotations **@Mock** and **@InjectMocks** come from Mockito. The **@Mock** designates a mock object, while **@InjectMocks** instructs Mockito to create a real instance of **BookService** and inject the mock into it. The call to **when(...).thenReturn(...)** sets up the behavior of the mock repository. The tests confirm that the service logic returns the expected results. No real database is involved, so these tests run quickly and deterministically.

Advanced Mockito Patterns

The Mockito also supports verifying interactions. Let us say that your service calls a repository method exactly once. You can write:

```
verify(repository, times(1)).findById(anyLong());
```

This line checks that **findById** was indeed called once with any **Long** parameter, detecting unintentional multiple calls. For stateful logic, you might chain mocks or handle partial mocking. If a method calls an external service that you do not want to replicate, mocking or stubbing with **@MockBean** in a Spring Boot test can isolate the code under test.

Test Organization and Best Practices

Keeping test classes parallel to their main classes aids discoverability. For **BookService.java** in **src/main/java**, **BookServiceTest.java** might reside in **src/test/java**. Each test class can focus on one target class, ensuring clarity in purpose. If a method is particularly complex, consider multiple test methods covering distinct scenarios or error conditions.

Also, mocking everything can lead to over-isolation. Here, try to consider layering your tests, starting with unit tests for logic classes and continuing with integration tests for data-access code or external connections. A robust test suite includes a mix of both. Unit tests excel at verifying logic in isolation, while integration tests confirm that the entire stack—repositories, messaging, or HTTP calls—behaves as expected.

Debugging Failures

When a unit test doesn't work right, it'll often show a stack trace or an assertion error. That'll help you figure out what's going wrong by showing what the expected outcome is and where it's different from the actual outcome. If you're having trouble finding the root of the problem, modern IDEs let you set breakpoints in test code or debug sessions. You can also check out local variables to see if there's a missed edge case or a problem with mocking. For concurrency or asynchronous code, you might need to control threads or use advanced mocks. If you're aiming for code coverage, tools like JaCoCo or SonarQube can show which lines are being tested, helping you improve coverage.

In a CI environment, failing tests can block merges or deployments, encouraging teams to fix issues promptly. This makes the code better overall and stops minor bugs from spreading. And when you combine JUnit, Mockito, and a CI pipeline, you get quick feedback on code changes. If developers prioritize fixing broken tests, the codebase will become more reliable over time.

Beyond unit tests, verifying entire microservices might involve integration tests with in-memory databases or test containers. Another thing to keep in mind is contract testing. This makes sure that interactions between services match what was expected. End-to-end tests confirm how the user interacts with the system. But at the end of the day, unit tests are still the foundation. They give you the fastest feedback on changes to your local code. If you build a strong culture around these fundamentals, the GitforGits application will stay stable, easy to refactor, and free of unexpected regressions.

Integration Testing

Why Integration Testing?

After creating a robust suite of unit tests, it helps to confirm that your code interacts properly with external systems or internal components. An integration test checks multiple parts of the application, verifying that they behave together as expected. This method goes beyond mocking dependencies and actually involves real or simulated resources such as databases, message brokers, or HTTP services. By spotting mismatches in data formats, request routing, or transaction boundaries, integration tests reduce the risk of surprises when the application runs in production. Teams often place integration tests in a separate package or folder within **`src/test/java`**, isolating them from unit tests to manage complexity. Each test can spin up part of the environment, configure required services, and then run end-to-end scenarios. For microservices, integration testing can extend to verifying inter-service calls, or confirming that a local codebase communicates properly with a test instance of another service.

Setting up Testing Environment

Typically, integration tests might rely on an in-memory database for repositories, or use Docker-based containers for an actual database if your code demands strict parity with production. The Spring Boot test framework includes features like **`@SpringBootTest`**, which loads an entire application context, plus optional annotations for specifying active profiles or test properties.

For example:

```
@SpringBootTest
@ActiveProfiles("test")
class BookIntegrationTest {
    @Autowired
    private MockMvc mockMvc;
    @Autowired
    private BookRepository bookRepository;
    // tests
}
```

Here, the annotation loads a test context, letting you query beans, run HTTP endpoints via **MockMvc**, or perform data lookups in a test database. The **@ActiveProfiles("test")** means the application pulls configuration from **application-test.properties** or a Config Server test profile, ensuring it does not connect to production resources. If you rely on an in-memory database, the schema can be auto-created from your JPA entities, giving a fresh environment for each test. This strategy also prevents data contamination between tests.

Using MockMvc for HTTP-Level Tests

A frequent integration test pattern involves sending actual HTTP requests to controllers and verifying responses, bypassing the need for mocking frameworks. Spring Boot's **MockMvc** simulates inbound requests. For example:

```
@Test
void createBook_ShouldReturn201() throws Exception {
    String newBookJson = "{\"title\":\"Test
Book\",\"author\":\"Author\",\"isbn\":\"12345\"}";
    mockMvc.perform(post("/books")
              .contentType(MediaType.APPLICATION_JSON)
              .content(newBookJson))
           .andExpect(status().isCreated())
           .andExpect(jsonPath("$.title").value("Test Book"));
```

```
}
```

In the above code snippet, the test starts a servlet context, processes the **/books** endpoint, and checks the HTTP response. If the code interacts with a real database, that record is inserted. Another test can call **GET /books** to confirm the newly created entry is visible.

Testcontainers for External Services

Many projects rely on Docker-based Testcontainers to spin up ephemeral databases or message brokers. If your code interacts with Kafka, MySQL, or Redis, you can define a container in the test that automatically starts the relevant service.

For example, check the below sample program:

```
@Container
static MySQLContainer<?> mysql = new
MySQLContainer<>("mysql:8")
        .withDatabaseName("testdb")
        .withUsername("test")
        .withPassword("test");
@BeforeAll
static void setUpAll() {
    mysql.start();
    System.setProperty("spring.datasource.url",
mysql.getJdbcUrl());
    System.setProperty("spring.datasource.username",
mysql.getUsername());
    System.setProperty("spring.datasource.password",
mysql.getPassword());
}
```

When the test suite runs, MySQL is pulled and started in Docker. The application points to the container's JDBC URL automatically. After tests finish, the container stops. This pattern yields a closer match to production while still allowing automated local or CI runs. If the code uses a specialized feature, the container ensures that you test the actual service, not an approximation.

Multi-Service Integration

Microservices sometimes need to confirm that two or more services collaborate effectively. If you have a **`BookService`** and **`AuthorService`**, integration testing might involve launching both with Testcontainers or separate local processes. The test ensures that a "create book" request triggers the correct interaction with **`AuthorService`**. Alternatively, you can run a single service in the test but point it to a test double or partial real environment for the other. Another approach is to adopt consumer-driven contract testing (e.g., Pact) to verify that each service meets the agreed-upon API. The method you choose depends on your architecture and time constraints.

Here are some of the best practices that we can recommend for this type of testing:

- Keep integration tests targeted. Each test can focus on one scenario or flow, rather than an exhaustive sequence. If the code is small, fewer integration tests might suffice.
- Use naming conventions like "shouldCreateBook_WhenPostValidData" to reflect both the action and expected outcome.
- Expand coverage incrementally. Start with critical paths, then add less-traveled flows over time.
- Watch logs for unexpected errors, as integration tests might uncover real misconfigurations, missing environment variables, or hidden dependencies.
- Leverage environment variables or test profiles to isolate secrets or credentials from production usage.

This testing strategy is like a trusty pair of glasses for your software — it'll help you avoid those pesky bugs and save you tons of time fixing problems after deployment. When you combine it with CI, integration tests can spot new issues quickly, so you can fix them right away and keep your app stable.

Debugging Techniques

If you're methodical about debugging, you won't waste as much time trying random things. Whether we're talking about microservices or monolithic backends, issues are bound to pop up: null pointers, faulty logic, performance bottlenecks, or misconfigurations. Each type of bug needs a different plan and tools. By using logs, debuggers, and even remote inspection, developers can find the flaws quickly. Having well-structured logs and cross-service correlation often shows how the system flows or where data becomes invalid. You can use a debugger to step through the code, and there are tools that target CPU usage or memory leaks. And if you use consistent patterns—like consistent correlation IDs or preconfigured log levels—it'll help you see more. A thorough debugging session might start by reproducing the error in a local environment, capturing relevant logs, and stepping line by line to confirm the actual state vs. the expected state. Once you've figured out the root cause, you can propose a fix, test it, and verify it in a staging environment before rolling it out.

Debugging with Logs and Correlation IDs

A typical first step in diagnosing a bug is checking logs to see if exceptions or warnings appear. In Spring Boot, adding code like:

```
private static final Logger logger =
LoggerFactory.getLogger(MyService.class);

public void processOrder(Order order) {

    logger.debug("Processing order with ID: {}",
order.getId());

    // ...

    logger.info("Order processed successfully: {}",
order.getId());

}
```

ensures essential information is recorded at various stages. If an exception emerges, the stack trace might show the failing class or method. For microservices, adopting correlation IDs helps unify logs across services. A simple approach is to pass a header like **X-Correlation-ID** from one service to another, storing it in a ThreadLocal or using something like Spring Cloud Sleuth.

Next, each log line can include the correlation ID:

```
logging.pattern.level=%5p [%X{correlationId}]
```

As a result, searching logs for a specific correlation ID reveals the entire request flow. If the code logs any unexpected data or a stack trace, it becomes easier to see how it traveled among microservices.

Using IDE Debugger

IDEs like IntelliJ or Eclipse let developers set breakpoints in the code, even in frameworks like Spring Boot. For example, if a **BookController** fails to return the correct data, place a breakpoint on the method:

```
@RestController

@RequestMapping("/books")

public class BookController {

    @GetMapping("/{id}")

    public Book getBook(@PathVariable Long id) {
```

```
        // place breakpoint here
        return bookService.findBook(id);
    }
}
```

When running the project in debug mode, stepping into **bookService.findBook(id)** reveals the actual parameters, return objects, and thrown exceptions. This technique confirms whether the repository query returns an unexpected result or if an NPE occurs. If the environment is remote, you can pass **-agentlib:jdwp=transport=dt_socket,server=y,suspend=n,address=5005** as a JVM argument, then attach the IDE debugger. The monitoring of variable states in real time can pinpoint exactly where data becomes incorrect. For concurrency issues, stepping through threads or using breakpoints that trigger on specific conditions (e.g., variable changes) can reveal race conditions.

Leveraging Trace Tools for Distributed Systems

In a microservices environment, an error might appear in **BillingService** but originate in **OrderService**. There are various tools like Zipkin or Jaeger that can track distributed traces. By adding dependencies such as Spring Cloud Sleuth, each service automatically appends trace and span IDs to logs and external calls:

```
<dependency>
    <groupId>org.springframework.cloud</groupId>
    <artifactId>spring-cloud-starter-sleuth</artifactId>
    <version>3.1.5</version>
</dependency>
```

When a request enters **OrderService**, the application starts a trace. Subsequent calls to **BillingService** or **InventoryService** share the same trace ID. Observing the timeline in Zipkin shows each service's segments. If a particular call is too slow or returns an error, the trace clarifies exactly which microservice or method took the longest. This is especially helpful for tricky issues like partial failures, timeouts, or load-related slowdowns.

Sample Program: Logging Exception with Extra Data

Sometimes a service needs to include more context in logs:

```
try {
```

```
    // business logic
} catch (DatabaseException e) {
    logger.error("Failed to process record with userId={} due
to {}",
                 userId, e.getMessage(), e);
    throw e;
}
```

In the above, the code logs the userId and the full exception stack. Searching logs for **userId=123** helps confirm that the code encountered a DatabaseException. If you suspect a concurrency bug, increasing the log level to **DEBUG** on relevant classes might clarify whether multiple threads update the same record concurrently.

Performance or Memory Profiling

Some bugs manifest as slow responses or out-of-memory errors. Tools like VisualVM or Eclipse MAT can attach to a running JVM. A quick CPU sampling might show that **BookRepository.findAll()** is called 500 times when only 50 were expected. A memory histogram might reveal thousands of unused **List<Book>** instances. Checking code reveals a data structure that never gets cleared, leading to a memory leak. Given below is an example snippet:

```
public List<Book> bigCache = new ArrayList<>();
public void storeBooks(List<Book> books) {
    bigCache.addAll(books); // never removed
}
```

During normal usage, this grows unbounded, consuming memory. A memory profiler highlight such accumulations. Fixing the code might involve clearing **bigCache** after use or adopting a more controlled caching policy.

Sample Program: Debugging a Failing Integration Test

Suppose an integration test fails with a 500 error from **/books/{id}**. Checking the logs might show a **NullPointerException** in **BookService**. The debugger reveals that **repository.findById(id)** returns null. Observing the real database or container reveals that the table lacks the record. Possibly the test data was never inserted. The fix might involve seeding a test fixture:

```
@BeforeEach
void initData() {
    bookRepository.save(new Book("TestTitle", "Author", 1L));
}
```

Then the code works. This scenario demonstrates a common debugging pattern: logs indicate a 500, the debugger shows a null pointer, data is missing. A test fixture or data setup solves the root cause.

Continuous Integration and Delivery

It takes more than good code to deliver a stable backend. CI merges code changes a lot, automatically building and testing them. Continuous Delivery (CD) takes this a step further by automating deployments. This ensures that whenever code passes tests, it can be released to staging or production with minimal hassle. When teams adopt CI/CD pipelines, they cut down on manual steps that can lead to errors, keep test coverage high, and speed up feedback cycles. These pipelines usually run on tools like Jenkins, GitLab CI, GitHub Actions, or Bitbucket Pipelines, which orchestrate builds, tests, and deployments according to a configured script.

Setting up CI Pipeline

A typical pipeline compiles the code, runs unit and integration tests, checks code style or coverage, and if everything succeeds, archives or packages the artifact for possible deployment. In GitHub Actions, for instance, a **`.github/workflows/ci.yml`** file might define:

```
name: CI
on:
  push:
    branches: [ "main" ]
jobs:
  build-and-test:
    runs-on: ubuntu-latest
    steps:
      - name: Checkout
        uses: actions/checkout@v2
```

```
    - name: Set up JDK 11
      uses: actions/setup-java@v2
      with:
        java-version: '11'
    - name: Build with Maven
      run: mvn clean install
```

When new commits push to the **main** branch, GitHub triggers this workflow. The pipeline checks out code, sets up Java 11, then runs **mvn clean install**. If unit tests or integration tests fail, the pipeline halts, and the developer sees an error. Additional steps might run code coverage or linting. If the build passes, the pipeline can upload the artifact to a repository or store them as build artifacts for later retrieval.

Adding Integration Tests to Pipeline

The microservices might rely on Docker containers or advanced test steps. A snippet to run Testcontainers or Docker Compose could appear as below:

```
- name: Run tests with Docker Compose
  run: docker-compose -f docker-compose.test.yml up --build --
abort-on-container-exit
```

This above sets up dependent services like kafka so integration tests pass. The pipeline ensures that real or near-real environment testing remains part of the process, catching regressions that unit tests alone might miss. A second job might tag and publish Docker images if the build passes, storing them in an artifact registry for deployment.

Implementing CD for Automated Deployments

The CD extends the pipeline to push successful builds to a staging or production environment once manual or automatic approvals occur. We can make use of Jenkins or GitLab CI to run scripts that log in to a cluster or cloud environment, deploy the new artifact, and run acceptance tests.

For example, a Jenkins pipeline might have a stage:

```
stage('Deploy to Staging') {
    steps {
```

```
        sh "kubectl set image deployment/book-service book-service=myrepo/book-service:${env.BUILD_NUMBER}"
        sh "kubectl rollout status deployment/book-service"
    }
}
```

This snippet updates the **book-service** container image in Kubernetes to the newly built version. The pipeline then waits for the rollout to succeed. If staging tests pass, a final "Promote to Production" stage might do the same with a production cluster.

Managing Environment-specific Config

If the project uses a Config Server or environment variables, the pipeline can inject them for each environment. For instance, passing different **SPRING_PROFILES_ACTIVE** or **DATABASE_URL** ensures that the same code runs with environment-specific details. The pipeline might store secrets in an encrypted vault or in a repository's secret manager. A typical approach is to define environment variables in the CI/CD system, referencing them in the deployment script.

For example:

```
- name: Deploy
  env:
    SPRING_PROFILES_ACTIVE: production
    DB_PASSWORD: ${{ secrets.DB_PASSWORD }}
  run: ./deploy.sh
```

This above approach ensures the pipeline remains secure and flexible. If the DB password changes, updating the secret in the CI/CD platform suffices.

Monitoring and Rollbacks

A CD pipeline also includes post-deployment steps to verify success, such as health checks or smoke tests. If a new version fails after deployment, an automated rollback might restore the previous version. Tools like Kubernetes or advanced rolling deployment strategies can revert with minimal downtime. This practice ensures a faulty build does not linger in production. Observing logs or metrics can confirm that error rates or latencies remain stable after each deployment. By collecting these results, the pipeline might automatically approve or revert a deployment based on real-time performance signals.

Sample Program: Jenkinsfile for a Microservice

Below is a simplified Jenkinsfile program:

```
pipeline {
    agent any
    stages {
        stage('Checkout') {
            steps {
                checkout scm
            }
        }
        stage('Build & Test') {
            steps {
                sh 'mvn clean install'
            }
        }
        stage('Integration Tests') {
            steps {
                sh 'mvn verify -Pintegration'
            }
        }
        stage('Docker Build & Push') {
            when {
                branch 'main'
            }
            steps {
                sh 'docker build -t myrepo/book-
service:${BUILD_NUMBER} .'
                sh 'docker push myrepo/book-
service:${BUILD_NUMBER}'
```

```
            }
        }
        stage('Deploy to Staging') {
            steps {
                sh 'kubectl set image deployment/book-service
book-service=myrepo/book-service:${BUILD_NUMBER}'
                sh 'kubectl rollout status deployment/book-
service'
            }
        }
    }
}
```

This file is set up to run on code changes, do tests, build a Docker image, push to a registry, and deploy to a staging environment. You can also promote from staging to production by taking additional steps or using separate pipelines. All these steps automate tasks that might've needed manual intervention or ad-hoc scripts in the past.

Summary

In short, this chapter showed us that effective testing and debugging are key to making sure backend applications are solid. You explored how unit tests, written with JUnit and Mockito, isolated small pieces of logic and validated them in controlled scenarios. By mocking external dependencies, these tests ran quickly, revealed logic flaws, and prevented unexpected interactions with real systems. Then, we moved on to integration tests, which built on that by verifying how services worked together. To do this, they often spun up containers or in-memory databases to confirm that each service worked properly. You also checked out debugging strategies, mixing logs, breakpoints, and distributed tracing tools. Thorough logs and correlation IDs provided visibility into request paths, while IDE debuggers stepped through code to pinpoint missteps.

You then realized the importance of a step-by-step approach to fixing problems. Observing logs, analyzing stack traces, or attaching a remote debugger helped narrow down failing code paths. Profiling helped tackle performance issues by revealing slow methods or memory leaks. By keeping a consistent process, we could quickly reproduce and fix problems. With CI and delivery pipelines, these techniques minimized risk, so each new release had confidence that the code had passed multiple layers of validation. This made everything more stable and sped up development cycles.

CHAPTER 12: DEPLOYING JAVA BACKEND APPLICATIONS

Preparing App for Deploy

You can't just write code and be done. If you're building a production-grade Java app, you've got to do more. Each microservice or monolith has to handle traffic, log events, manage resources, and stay fault-tolerant in real-world environments. So, when you're getting ready to deploy, it's a good idea to optimize the build, minimize startup times, refine configurations, and make sure your GitforGits application meets the performance and security standards. No matter if you're thinking of deploying on virtual machines, container platforms, or a cloud environment, adopting certain best practices can help you avoid surprises once your users start hitting your service. This section's got some practical tips, like checking resource usage, packaging your app, and making sure the code's ready for production.

Choosing Right Build Artifacts

So, when you're working on a stable application build, you often start with something you can reproduce, like a fat JAR or a Docker image. For Spring Boot, generating an executable JAR is a piece of cake as below:

```
mvn clean package
```

If the **`pom.xml`** includes the Spring Boot Maven plugin, it wraps dependencies into one JAR. This format suits smaller deployments, letting you run the app with **`java -jar`**. Alternatively, containerizing your application might be more flexible. Using a Dockerfile:

```
FROM openjdk:17-jdk
ARG JAR_FILE=target/gitforgits.jar
COPY ${JAR_FILE} app.jar
ENTRYPOINT ["java","-jar","/app.jar"]
```

Once built, the Docker image encapsulates the entire runtime. This approach ensures consistent environments and easy scaling in container orchestrators like Kubernetes. If your system uses multiple microservices, each might produce its own image, referencing the same base image or a specialized variant (like distroless or alpine) for smaller footprints.

Optimizing Configuration

Spring Boot and Java offer numerous configuration settings that impact performance. For instance, adjusting the JVM's heap size to match your hardware or container memory prevents out-of-memory crashes. If a typical container has 512MB, set **`-Xmx256m`** or something appropriate. The **`spring.datasource`** properties can refine database pooling. If concurrency is high, increasing pool sizes might help, though it also consumes more memory.

Meanwhile, ensuring that **spring.jpa.hibernate.ddl-auto** is not set to **create** or **update** in production avoids accidental schema changes. If you use the Config Server, each environment's profile might store production credentials or advanced caching settings. Confirm that no debugging features remain active. For example, disabling **spring.jpa.show-sql** and lowering logging levels reduce overhead.

Preparing Database and External Dependencies

And before shipping the code, it's a good idea to make sure that your production databases are seeded or migrated. That way, you can avoid any data mismatch. There are tools like Flyway or Liquibase that can help with managing schema changes across different environments. And if your microservices use message brokers, caches, or external APIs, make sure they're set up in production with the right credentials. For Redis caching, a production-grade Redis cluster might be different from the single-node local version. And don't forget to double-check your TLS settings, firewall rules, and host addresses. If you're using Kafka, make sure your topic structure is set up or migrated.

Logging and Monitoring

Production environments often log selectively at **INFO** or **WARN** levels, limiting debug data. However, each microservice or module should still produce enough logs to explore errors. Tools like ELK Stack or Splunk gather logs from each container or VM, letting your team search or filter them easily. Incorporating a correlation ID or a trace ID fosters cross-service debugging. If you adopt Spring Cloud Sleuth or similar tracing, configure it so that production logs contain minimal overhead but remain traceable. For metrics, hooking into tools like Prometheus or Graphite captures CPU usage, memory consumption, request latencies, and error rates. Building dashboards helps detect abnormal spikes or slowdowns. If you spot high load, you can scale horizontally—assuming your application is stateless or well-partitioned—preventing user-facing slowdowns or downtime.

Security Considerations

Shifting from development to production demands secure configurations. If the application uses OAuth2 or session-based authentication, ensuring TLS is active on all public endpoints is vital. Self-signed certificates might suffice for testing, but production typically requires valid certificates from a CA. If your microservices communicate internally, consider secure channels or a service mesh if the data is sensitive. Checking that secrets like database passwords or API keys are not stored in the code or logs is crucial. Instead, environment variables, secrets managers, or the Config Server handle them. If your environment demands compliance (e.g., GDPR, PCI DSS), logging PII requires extra care. Minimizing open ports and adopting a firewall strategy can close vulnerabilities. Each microservice might only expose the ports required for actual traffic, especially if you have a gateway for external routes.

Deployment Options

You might use a JAR or Docker container if you're using bare-metal servers or VMs. Tools like systemd or Windows services can run the process when the computer boots up. A more modern approach is container orchestration with Kubernetes or Docker Swarm. With Kubernetes, you define deployment manifests specifying your container image, environment variables, and resource limits:

```
apiVersion: apps/v1
kind: Deployment
metadata:
  name: gitforgits
spec:
  replicas: 2
  selector:
    matchLabels:
      app: gitforgits
  template:
    metadata:
      labels:
        app: gitforgits
    spec:
      containers:
      - name: gitforgits-app
        image: myrepo/gitforgits:latest
        ports:
        - containerPort: 8080
        resources:
          limits:
            memory: "512Mi"
            cpu: "500m"
```

This file ensures two replicas run, each limited to half a CPU and 512MB memory. Kubernetes automatically restarts them if they crash or an update occurs. Cloud providers like AWS ECS, Azure AKS, or Google GKE manage containers similarly, each offering integrated load balancing. If the application uses advanced features like config maps or secrets, you can mount them at runtime. In microservices environments, the Eureka server or config server might also run in containers.

Final Verification before Launch

As the date approaches for a production release, a final checklist might confirm that logs, metrics, and alarms are in place. Security scans or static analysis can highlight known vulnerabilities or outdated dependencies. A staging environment that mirrors production sets the stage for a dress rehearsal. Running a short traffic test or partial canary release confirms if new changes behave under real loads. After successful validations, flipping traffic to the new version or performing a rolling update completes the transition. If issues arise, a rollback plan—like deploying the previous container image—provides safety. This plan ensures your users experience minimal disruption while receiving the updated application.

Each aspect—caching, concurrency settings, environment profiles, or container orchestration—plays a role in guaranteeing reliability and performance. Although the initial setup might seem extensive, these best practices pay off by reducing downtime, preventing runtime surprises, and forming a foundation for steady growth. With a well-prepared codebase, supportive CI/CD pipelines, and robust environment management, the jump to production can be smooth and confident.

Deploying to Application Servers

Understanding Tomcat

Tomcat is a servlet container that can host Java web applications by loading WAR files (Web Application Archive). When building a Spring Boot application, packaging as a WAR file instead of the usual JAR is one route. Alternatively, if the application is still packaged as a JAR, it can embed Tomcat internally, so direct deployment on an external Tomcat might require adjusting a bit. If you plan to rely on an external Tomcat instance, consider disabling Spring Boot's embedded Tomcat and generating a WAR. That approach leaves Tomcat as the main container, controlling the lifecycle. The environment typically has Tomcat installed on a server, listening on port 8080 or 80. The WAR is dropped into Tomcat's **`webapps`** directory or deployed via the Tomcat Manager.

Building WAR for GitforGits

A standard Spring Boot application might produce a JAR by default. Converting it to a WAR involves adjusting the **pom.xml**. For instance:

```
<packaging>war</packaging>
<dependencies>
    <!-- Exclude embedded Tomcat and rely on external
container -->
    <dependency>
        <groupId>org.springframework.boot</groupId>
        <artifactId>spring-boot-starter-tomcat</artifactId>
        <scope>provided</scope>
    </dependency>
</dependencies>
```

A main class typically extends **SpringBootServletInitializer** to support WAR deployment:

```
@SpringBootApplication
public class GitforGitsApplication extends
SpringBootServletInitializer {
    @Override
    protected SpringApplicationBuilder
configure(SpringApplicationBuilder builder) {
        return builder.sources(GitforGitsApplication.class);
    }
    public static void main(String[] args) {
        SpringApplication.run(GitforGitsApplication.class,
args);
    }
}
```

Once configured, running **mvn clean package** yields a WAR file named something like **gitforgits.war** inside the **target** folder. This WAR is the artifact that Tomcat can host. If the environment uses an older Java EE structure, adopting a **web.xml** might be necessary for advanced scenarios, but Spring Boot often runs with zero or minimal changes.

Deploying WAR to Tomcat

After building the WAR, place it into Tomcat's **webapps/** directory. Suppose the WAR is named **gitforgits.war**. On startup, Tomcat expands the WAR into a folder named **gitforgits**, making the application accessible at **http://server-host:8080/gitforgits/**.

Another approach is using the Tomcat Manager. If Tomcat Manager is enabled, logging in to **http://server-host:8080/manager/html** reveals a form to upload the WAR or specify a remote URL. Deployment is immediate once the file is processed. The manager can also handle restarts or undeploy actions. If logs are needed, checking the **logs/** folder in Tomcat (e.g., **catalina.out** or **localhost.log**) captures startup messages or errors. Confirm that the Spring context loads and no exceptions surface. The environment variables or system properties can pass in configuration data. For instance, if the application needs a certain profile:

```
export SPRING_PROFILES_ACTIVE=production
catalina.sh run
```

The environment can also store secrets or DB credentials. If the code relies on the Config Server, it might be enough to define **-Dspring.cloud.config.uri=**. On multi-instance servers, each instance might deploy its own WAR with a unique context path, or a single Tomcat might handle many microservices. Keep memory constraints in mind—if multiple WARs run, the server's heap usage accumulates. Tools like **server.xml** or **context.xml** help define advanced configurations, including JNDI data sources or SSL connectors.

Testing and Managing Deployment

After placing the WAR, verifying that the GitforGits app runs as expected is essential. Checking endpoints with **curl** or a browser confirms that the correct content loads. If any environment variable is missing, Spring might throw exceptions at startup. If concurrency is high, analyzing the Tomcat thread pool or concurrency settings might optimize throughput. The default thread pool can be set in **server.xml** with something like:

```
<Executor name="tomcatThreadPool" namePrefix="catalina-exec-"
          maxThreads="200" minSpareThreads="10"/>
```

Matching these settings to the application's concurrency usage ensures no unexpected bottlenecks. If integrated with a load balancer, each Tomcat node might handle requests behind a round-robin or weighted policy, allowing horizontal scaling. Over time, logs in **catalina.out** or custom log files help diagnose performance issues. The manager console can also display memory usage or request stats; though advanced setups might place an APM agent in the server.

Containerization with Docker

Installing Docker and Basic Commands

Containers wrap the application and all dependencies—like the JVM, libraries, and configuration—into a single image that runs consistently anywhere Docker is installed. This ensures no mismatch in OS libraries, no manual steps, and simpler scaling. Instead of configuring Tomcat or environment variables on each server manually, the Docker image holds everything needed to start the application. If additional microservices appear, each can have its own container, orchestrated by Docker tools or a platform like Kubernetes. Using containers also speeds up local development. A developer can run **docker-compose** to spin up a database, message broker, and the app, replicating a near-production environment. This standardization shrinks the gap between dev, staging, and production, making deployment consistent.

A typical Linux environment installs Docker using commands like:

```
sudo apt-get update
sudo apt-get install docker.io
sudo systemctl enable docker
sudo systemctl start docker
```

Confirming Docker works might involve checking **docker --version**. Running **docker run hello-world** verifies that containers function. If it outputs a friendly greeting, Docker is active. By default, the user might need privileges to run Docker commands, or be part of the **docker** group. Then building images and pushing them to a registry becomes straightforward.

Creating Dockerfile

Spring Boot's JAR approach simplifies containerization. The official **openjdk** images supply a base. A typical Dockerfile might look like:

```
FROM openjdk:17-jdk-alpine
VOLUME /tmp
ARG JAR_FILE=target/gitforgits.jar
COPY ${JAR_FILE} app.jar
EXPOSE 8080
ENTRYPOINT ["java","-jar","/app.jar"]
```

If the JAR is named **gitforgits-1.0.jar**, specifying **ARG JAR_FILE=target/gitforgits-1.0.jar** or adjusting to match your build. The **EXPOSE 8080** line signals that the container listens on port 8080. The **ENTRYPOINT** instructs Docker to run the jar.

To build the image:

```
mvn clean package
docker build -t gitforgits:latest .
```

Then start a container:

```
docker run -d -p 8080:8080 --name gitforgits-container
gitforgits:latest
```

Visiting **http://localhost:8080** shows the application. The container logs are accessible via **docker logs gitforgits-container**. If environment variables are needed:

```
docker run -d -p 8080:8080 -e
SPRING_PROFILES_ACTIVE=production gitforgits:latest
```

It'll pass those environment variables to the JVM. The same goes if the app calls external services. Just configure them as environment variables or link containers with Docker networks.

Persisting Data and Volumes

If the application uses a local file system for data (like uploads), mapping a Docker volume preserves data across restarts. Let us take an example:

```
VOLUME /uploads
```

Then a Compose file might define a volume:

```
services:
  gitforgits-app:
    volumes:
      - app-uploads:/uploads
volumes:
  app-uploads:
```

This confirms that container ephemeral storage is not lost. A production environment might rely on external object stores or databases, but sometimes local volumes remain enough for small scale. The key is ensuring that ephemeral containers do not lose critical data with each redeploy.

Building Minimal Images

Some organizations prefer minimal base images to reduce security risks. For instance, shifting from **openjdk:17-jdk-alpine** to a distroless image or a custom OS might lower the final image size. The trade-off is a narrower debugging environment—some distroless images lack common shell tools. Using multi-stage builds can help produce small final images:

```
FROM maven:3.8.4-openjdk-17 as build
WORKDIR /app
COPY . .
RUN mvn clean package -DskipTests
FROM openjdk:17-jdk-alpine
COPY --from=build /app/target/gitforgits.jar /app.jar
ENTRYPOINT ["java","-jar","/app.jar"]
```

In the above code snippet, the first stage compiles code. The second stage copies only the finished JAR, yielding a smaller final image.

Deploying Containers

Once images are built, pushing them to a registry like Docker Hub or a private registry helps distribute them. Take an example:

```
docker tag gitforgits:latest myrepo/gitforgits:latest
docker push myrepo/gitforgits:latest
```

A production cluster (like Kubernetes) references that image:

```
apiVersion: apps/v1
kind: Deployment
metadata:
  name: gitforgits-deployment
spec:
```

```
replicas: 2
template:
  spec:
    containers:
    - name: gitforgits
      image: myrepo/gitforgits:latest
      ports:
      - containerPort: 8080
```

In the above, the kubernetes pulls **`myrepo/gitforgits:latest`**, spinning up two pods. The same principle applies if using AWS ECS, Azure Container Instances, or Docker Swarm.

Logging and Monitoring in Containers

By default, container logs go to standard output. There are a few tools out there, such as docker logs or the orchestrator's logging driver, that you could use to capture them. A separate service might forward them to Elasticsearch or Splunk. If you need more advanced monitoring, you can add a sidecar container or agent. For example, if the app has to run a collector or if you attach a Prometheus JMX exporter, you might need this. Since logs disappear once a container stops, it's crucial to externalize them for troubleshooting.

There are some best practices that I have tried to gather, like:

- Keep Dockerfiles simple, layering minimal logic so caching works effectively.
- Do not store secrets in the image; pass them at runtime as environment variables or use secret managers.
- Adopt a standard for tagging images (like semantic versions or commit SHAs) for traceability and rollback.
- Ensure local dev environments match production images, so fewer "works on my machine" issues arise.
- Combine containerization with CI/CD, so building and pushing images is part of the pipeline, guaranteeing consistent deployments.

Just combine Docker with your current testing pipelines, microservices architectures, and environment setups, and the GitforGits project can adapt to many deployment targets while keeping overhead minimal.

Summary

So, that's a wrap for our last chapter. In this chapter, you learned how to set up an app for production, make sure it runs smoothly, handles logs properly, and can handle real traffic. You also figured out how to optimize configurations, like adjusting JVM heap sizes or setting environment-specific properties, and making sure caches and concurrency settings matched actual loads. You also learned about the importance of good logging and monitoring practices, like collecting metrics and using external log aggregators to track performance and error rates. You also learned about containerization and using an external Tomcat to deliver your code in a consistent and maintainable way.

You also learned how each part of the system, like databases or message queues, contributes to a successful deployment. You also learned how to adapt environment variables, Docker images, or specialized profiles to make the application behave in various stages, like dev, staging, or production. Then, you checked out horizontal scaling, load testing, and advanced security settings like TLS or secrets management. Finally, to make sure everything was working right, you made sure that CI/CD pipelines were building stable artifacts, testing them, and rolling them out without any manual interference. This whole process really drives home the idea that a well-prepared application not only launches smoothly but also stays strong and simple to update as needs grow.

Index

A

B

C

D

E

F

G

H

I

J

K

L

M

O

P

R

S

T

U

V

W

Y

Z

Epilogue

The lessons in this book are designed to help you apply what you've learned to your daily coding adventures, not just to sit on the shelf. Each concept, from building user-friendly APIs to caching results, is something you can use in your daily coding endeavors. If you're struggling with performance issues, no worries! You can find helpful tips in the caching chapter or the concurrency details to improve your throughput. And when it's time for something new, you can count on strategies like continuous integration and container deployment to roll out updates smoothly. And when the security team has some concerns, you can turn to the steps on user authentication or encryption in transit for guidance.

And if you're ever unsure, no worries! The comprehensive approach to configuring microservices, integrating them into a discovery system, and connecting them to a gateway is like a safety net, ensuring that your services can evolve independently no matter what. And of course, testing, debugging, and logging are still super important as your application grows. This book shows you that each skill works really well with the others. It's all about working together: observing logs in real time, orchestrating containers, or spinning up ephemeral test environments, all coming together to give you a development cycle that flows smoothly. I hope that by revisiting chapters whenever you encounter new challenges, you'll keep finding helpful techniques, allowing your daily Java projects to flourish with minimal confusion and maximum success.

- ***Elara Drevyn***

Thank You

www.ingramcontent.com/pod-product-compliance
Lightning Source LLC
Chambersburg PA
CBHW080214170726
48282CB00030B/1108
9788197950452